Malcolm E. Shaw is President of Educational Systems & Designs, Inc., consultants in management and organization development and in public administration.

Emmett Wallace is a Vice President of Educational Systems & Designs, Inc., and serves as a consultant to many business, educational, governmental, and voluntary organizations in the United States and overseas.

Frances N. LaBella is a Vice President of Educational Systems & Designs, Inc., and has been engaged in the development of programs in management, communications, and organization development.

MAKING IT, ASSERTIVELY

Malcolm E. Shaw
Emmett Wallace, Ph.D
Frances N. LaBella
Educational Systems & Designs Inc.

A SPECTRUM BOOK

PRENTICE-HALL, INC., Englewood Cliffs, N.J. 07632

Library of Congress Cataloging in Publication Data

SHAW, MALCOLM E
   Making it, assertively.

   (A Spectrum Book)
   1.–Assertiveness (Psychology)   2.–Assertiveness
(Psychology)—Problems, exercises, etc.   I.–Wallace,
Emmett, joint author.   II.–LaBella, Frances N.,
joint author.   III.–Title.
BF575.A85S5   158′.1   80–19406
ISBN 0–13–545897–8
ISBN 0–13–545889–7 (pbk.)

A SPECTRUM BOOK

10 9 8 7 6 5 4 3 2 1

Printed in the United States of America

PRENTICE-HALL INTERNATIONAL, INC., *London*
PRENTICE-HALL OF AUSTRALIA PTY. LIMITED, *Sydney*
PRENTICE-HALL OF CANADA, LTD., *Toronto*
PRENTICE-HALL OF INDIA PRIVATE LIMITED, *New Delhi*
PRENTICE-HALL OF JAPAN, INC., *Tokyo*
PRENTICE-HALL OF SOUTHEAST ASIA PTE. LTD., *Singapore*
WHITEHALL BOOKS LIMITED, *Wellington, New Zealand*

CONTENTS

FOREWORD

The need to survive and grow is a universal human characteristic. In our need to survive, we must learn to defend ourselves. In our need to grow, we must learn to use the resources of others. Unfortunately, in the process of defending ourselves or of increasing our impact, we often diminish others. The diminishment of others is so commonplace in our society that many of us have come to accept oppression and victimization as inevitable. We have come to accept oppression as inexplicably involved with leadership and victim-hood as a state of affairs in which the individual has no choices.

This book makes two significant points that lead us to consider two alternative ways of thinking on these matters:

1. It points to ways in which one can be forceful, firm and impactful without diminishing others.
2. It makes it clear that no one has to be a victim in open, democratically-oriented societies unless he or she chooses to do so.

My work in both organization and community development in a wide variety of settings has convinced me that mature, effective people—regardless of attributes of race, gender and ethnicity—accept these insights as principles. Wholesome and effective people know that they can win without creating losers. They know that they are responsible for their own behavior and they have the capacity and the right to defend their interests.

This book sheds light on how we can increase our capacity to grow and survive while at the same time avoiding the potential pitfalls of becoming oppressor or victim.

Elaine D. Carter

Elaine Carter is President of Elaine Carter Associates, Inc., consultants in organization development and specialists in minority group relations.

PREFACE

Literally dozens of books have been written during recent years on being more assertive. So why another one? We feel that this book is different: that it treats assertiveness from a somewhat different and more holistic (total) perspective and that it helps the reader to identify concrete and practical steps towards personal improvement.

We want this preface to be as useful to the reader as the body of the book. Here, then, is a summary of this book's distinctive features, some of which may be shared by other books, but all of which are contained in no other book on assertiveness to the best of our knowledge.

This book is for everyone. Concern about assertiveness originally developed from interest in Women's Liberation and a desire to promote female assertiveness. The literature has become more universal, though most assertiveness training programs continue to attract a predominance of females and, to an increasing extent, members of minority groups. It is our conviction that learning to become more assertive is much more widely applicable. It is useful for those who are aggressive as well as those who are nonassertive—for men and women, executives and supervisors, in business and government, professional and technical personnel, union leaders, community leaders, educators, and church leaders. These are some of the populations with which we have worked as we developed the concepts and techniques presented in this book.

This book emphasizes assertiveness as a two-way, interactive process. Practically all of the books to date have urged the individual to go after what he/she wants, to express his/her feelings without guilt or apology. We do too. But we also emphasize that this should be done with a sensitivity and responsiveness towards others that recognizes their rights. The aim is to draw on our resources together with the resources of others in order to achieve mutually satisfactory ends.

This book shows how a rational, problem-solving approach can help make you more assertive. To be effectively assertive you need not only to be able to express your feelings, wants, and needs, but you have to be clear about your goals and how you expect to achieve them. So we suggest ways you can use problem-solving techniques to become more impactful and influential.

This is a "how-to-do-it" book. Although it draws on what has been learned from psychology, it is a practical guide to improving your performance. Dozens of examples are presented to illustrate "right" and "wrong" approaches.

This book provides tools for self-improvement. Self-analysis questionnaires and self-improvement guides are provided so that you will be able to pursue your own step-by-step program to become more assertive. Activities and techniques are suggested to enable you to practice being more assertive and to improve your capacities. This book, then, can engage you in an active learning process.

Thanks are due many individuals who have contributed to the concepts and techniques in this book: particularly Wallace Wohlking of the New York State School of Industrial and Labor Relations (Cornell), who first suggested that assertiveness training could be designed especially for managers; Pearl Rutledge, Ph.D., who originally trained us in assertiveness techniques and contributed to the development of Educational Systems and Design's initial programs; and Elaine Carter, a consultant in organizational behavior and social change, who has worked with us in adapting many of the techniques to specialized programs for minority groups. Susan Powley and Frances Butler typed and retyped the manuscript through its many revisions.

CHAPTER **1**

GOING AFTER
WHAT YOU WANT

During the last twenty-four hours you have gotten many things you wanted. Whether you simply asked someone to pass you the salt, convinced someone to go to a movie or restaurant that you prefer, or made some significant gain in your status or income, you have achieved results.

At this very moment, thinking about the last twenty-four hours, you are beginning to reveal to yourself some basic attitudes about your effectiveness. If the first thing that passes through your mind is the number of things you *didn't* get—how nasty or tough the world has been to you, how unappreciated or misunderstood you are—then the chances are good that you are not controlling your own destiny. If, on the other hand, you are able to think quickly and easily of specific small or large accomplishments, then there is a good chance you have a sound base upon which to build an increasingly effective mode for getting things done and achieving what you want.

The fact is that from the simplest act (getting someone to pass you the salt) to more demanding and complex situations (getting a higher level position) you are involved in influencing other people and in achieving results. The stakes may be higher in one situation than another but the fundamental process is the same. The basic steps are deceptively simple. The execution of these steps, however, requires knowledge, skill, and a great deal of practice.

FOUR STEPS

Perhaps most important of all, "getting what you want" requires you to be in touch with and aware of your own resources, your own strengths, and to accompany that awareness with a willingness to act. Nothing happens unless you are willing and able to take the following steps.

Know What You Want

Occasionally, individuals get unexpected windfalls: they inherit money, they get a promotion they were not seeking, they are discovered and move ahead without any overt effort on their own part. For every individual who has a fortunate experience of this kind, there are thousands who will not get what they want unless they identify what they want and make a specific effort to go after it. The actor who is "discovered," the sales representative or businessperson who suddenly starts making money, the individual who becomes popular and sought after, in almost every case has made a significant investment in him/herself and in pursuing his/her goals. *There is little chance of getting somewhere unless you know where you're going.* So the first step in the process is to acknowledge what you want.

Right now make a list of things you want. Consider relationships: Do you want more friends? Do you want to change your relationship with your spouse, your children, your boss? Consider achievement: Do you want to do more, make more sales, make more money, get a promotion? Consider your personal effectiveness: Do you want to be more forceful, more understanding, more respected?

Make your list—be specific:

I want:

_____

_____

_____

_____

_____

_____

_____

_____

Don't "Try"

One of the most frequently encountered obstacles to achievement is the "I'll give it a try" attitude versus the "I will do it" attitude. Assume, for example, that you want to get into an office to see someone who can aid you in your career or can arrange an important loan for you or provide you with needed information. One approach to reaching that person is to say to yourself, "I'm going to try to see Mr. X." Chances are that when you approach Mr. X's secretary your "I'll try" attitude will show through. If you approach the situation with the conviction that "I will see Mr. X" and direct your energy toward achievement of that end, your chances of succeeding are infinitely greater. There is obviously a delicate balance between self-possessed, confident behavior and cocky, egotistical behavior. The fact is you know the difference between being egotistical, overbearing, and aggressive versus being positive, constructive, and effectively forceful. (If you have any doubt as to whether you know the difference between these two sets of behavior, you will get a chance to look at them more closely in Chapter 2.)

Feel OK About Your Right to Act

There are many forces at work in your environment and past which will, unless you act, convince you that you have no right to go after what you want. *"You're too young"* or *"You're too old." "You're a woman,"* or *"You're black"* or *"You've never been to college,"* or *"Your family has never had money so why should you,"* or *"It's not nice to be acquisitive."* These and other "accidents" of birth, stereotypes, and folk tales can keep you from taking action. If you don't act there is *no* chance that you'll prevail.

If you look around you, you will find young and old, black and white, formally educated and self-educated, males and females making it. They are achieving what you may want to achieve—success, social ease, power, friendship, money, promotion. Whatever it is you want, others are getting it right now. It is not naive, wishful thinking to accept the fact that you have the right to pursue your goals. You may not prevail, you may not have the physical or mental gifts of a top performer in the field of your choice or you may encounter prejudice and resistance—you, nonetheless, have the right to go after what you want. If you want the salt, you have to ask someone to pass it. If you want a raise, a new career, new relationships, you have to pursue each goal. Ask for what you want, act on what you believe and from those processes you will either get what you want *or* learn more about yourself and how to modify your goals and plans.

Be Aware of the Other Person

Almost everything you want involves other people. Review the goals you set (see pages 61–62). What would you like to achieve in the next week, in the next six months—a raise, a promotion, an improved relationship with a friend or spouse, more respect from associates? If necessary expand your list.

As you examine that list, review each item and you will find that the achievement of almost every goal at some point involves other people. Even if your goals are "internalized" or self-oriented, for example, "I want to be smarter" or "a better musician" or "more self-assured," you need others to accomplish these goals. In part, you can achieve them by practice and self-study, but in large measure your success will depend upon interacting with others; obtaining support and interest from those who can help you learn what you want to learn, achieve what you want to achieve. Therefore, you must continuously be aware of the other person's resources and reactions.

IS THAT ALL?

It seems unbelievably simple—(1) Know what you want; (2) Don't try it—do it; (3) Accept that you have the right to act; (4) Be aware of others. As a matter of fact, each of these steps requires knowledge, skill, and practice. Each step requires the development of two basic capacities: the capacity to be assertive, not aggressive and the capacity to be responsive as opposed to nonassertive. The first step in the process of learning how to be more assertive and responsive is to clarify the nature of assertive, responsive, aggressive, and nonassertive behavior.

Definitions

Assertive: You are assertive when you express your opinions, goals, and wants clearly and without apologies or hostility. Assertiveness also involves standing up for your feelings, ideas, and your rights.

Aggressive: You are aggressive when you express your opinions, goals or wants in ways which demean or "put down" the feelings, ideas, or rights of others.

Nonassertive: You are nonassertive when you permit yourself to be demeaned or "put down" by others, when you react to others by being inappropriately apologetic or putting yourself down.

Responsive: You are responsive when you react to others by listening, by showing understanding, and by seeking out and responding to the ideas, feelings and opinions of others without demeaning yourself or putting yourself down.

THE NEXT STEP

The most effective way of becoming more assertive and affirmative, more responsive and involved is to use your resources—your knowledge and skills, your energy and drive, and your sensitivity. The chapters which follow will outline ways in which you can act upon your feelings and beliefs.

CHAPTER **2**

THAT'S RIGHT,
YOU'RE ASSERTIVE

In the last chapter you prepared a list indicating your goals and wants. As you think about that list, it will become clear that you have already achieved some of your purposes and are well on your way to achieving others. You have been able to get some of the things you want and you have let other people know where you stand and how you feel about things. You may not be as forceful or as affirmative as you'd like to be. You may, on the other hand, appear to be hard to get along with or abrasive. However, you do know how to be assertive even though you may not have consciously examined the way in which you get things done.

NATURE OF ASSERTIVENESS

Although you may feel assertive, although you have wants, drives and aspirations, although you may be aware of your rights as an individual and your unique resources, you are not assertive until you behave assertively. So the first element in the definition of assertiveness is that assertiveness is behavior. It requires action. When you are behaving assertively you express yourself, you let other people know what you're after, you take positions, you defend your rights and you act upon your beliefs.

It's important right at the start to recognize that it may not be appropriate to be assertive all of the time. There may be occasions when you need to defer action on some of your wants, needs or goals simply because you don't have the resources or background that will enable you to act decisively and achieve them. There may be times when you do not stand up for your rights or defend yourself simply because you're outgunned or overpowered. Later on, the conditions under which it is appropriate to act assertively will be examined more carefully.

Right now the key issue is to be sure that the nature of assertiveness is clear: assertive behavior is action. It requires you to express yourself, to go after things, to stand up for what you feel is right or necessary. Here are a few examples of assertive behavior to indicate the range of possibilities available to you as you move toward an increasingly assertive mode of action.

Saying No

When someone asks you to take on a committee responsibility or to do an unpleasant chore which is not part of your job, or to lend them money (when experience has shown that the person doesn't usually pay you back), you can assert yourself simply by saying "no." It is not necessary to apologize or give excuses, although it may be appropriate to explain your action. For example, you might say to someone asking you to do a special task, "I won't do that job now. I have other tasks which I must do in order to get my job done." Or, "No, I won't lend you money. I need all the cash I have." Or, "Until we settle the amount that's already owed, I don't want to have any more debts outstanding." There may be more effective, more pleasant ways of saying no; the main point is that one of your choices in behaving assertively is to refuse straightforwardly to take actions which you feel are not in your best interests or which are, for a variety of reasons, inappropriate.

You may choose, at times, to do things which are in response to the needs or concerns of others, your actions may be based on friendship or compassion. Assertiveness does not mean that you act only for yourself. It means that you do not ignore or deny your own needs, rights or feelings. It means you act in ways that do not diminish your own sense of worth. /

Defending Yourself Against Aggression or Personal Attacks

When someone "puts you down," insults you, or patronizes you, you have the right and capacity to assert yourself, to express your dissatisfaction with the behavior of the other and to take a stand regarding the issue at hand. For example, your boss might say to you, "Well, you're pretty new at the job and you don't have too good an education so I'm going to give you some simple assignments." Or, "We find that women don't carry out these jobs too well." Or, "We prefer to give these special tasks to people who are responsible." All of those statements are "putdowns." They imply that you lack responsibility or resources and they deny you an opportunity because of your sex or perhaps your age, race, or some other characteristic unrelated to performance. You have the right and capacity to assert yourself in these situations without becoming hostile or abrasive. So you might say, "I have the experience needed to do this task and I want to demonstrate what I can do." Or, "The fact that I'm a woman does not mean that I can't perform this task effectively. I can and will do it well."

Letting Others Know Where You Stand

The assertive act that is most often overlooked or avoided is one which involves going after what you want in a clear-cut and straightforward way. For example, assume you have some merchandise to return to a department store. You can act assertively by simply stating your goal or want: "I'm not satisfied with this merchandise and I want a cash refund." Note, in contrast, nonassertive behavior: "I'm awfully sorry to bother you and I don't know what your store's policy is, but it would be very nice and I'd certainly appreciate it if maybe you could give me my money back." Note, too, aggressive behavior: "I don't know what's wrong with this store. You people gave me the wrong merchandise and I think the clerk who handled it wasn't too bright, so you'd better give me my money back or I'm going to cause trouble." Similarly, when seeking a job or a promotion, a straightforward assertion is often appropriate: "I have the qualifications for the opening that exists." Or, "I am confident that I can carry out this job effectively."

Many experienced business people, actors and salespeople have found that it is appropriate to be clear about their own capacities and to go after what they want. For example, a top-level manager who feels qualified for a vice-presidential position often lets the boss know of this goal. The individual may say something like: "I want to become a vice-president of this organization and I'd like to discuss with you the steps I need to take in order to be ready for a top-level position in the future." Or, if the individual is already qualified, a simple statement of interest in the job and qualifications may suffice. Actors know that often the only way to get a part in a given play is to go after that part, to let the casting director know of their interest and capability. Similarly, teachers, nurses, and those who provide services, know that it is essential for them not to let the patient, student or client feel that the "service" person has no goals or wants of his/her own. So the nurse may need to say to the patient (or to an overly demanding doctor): "I'm working on an important activity and I want to continue working on it for the next half hour or so. Unless there's a serious emergency, please don't call me." Or the classroom teacher may need to say: "I want to present information about tomorrow's assignment that everyone should hear, so please be quiet."

There are more complicated forms of assertive behavior. However, the essence of assertiveness is contained in the examples that have been given. Assertive behavior lets people know where you stand, how you feel, or what you want; it makes it clear that you intend to stand up for your own rights and to defend yourself against exploitation or aggression. It is clear and expressive. If you are behaving assertively you are not "putting yourself down" (apologizing, demeaning yourself, or criticizing yourself) nor are you putting others down, acting in a hostile or abusive way, acting patronizing or contemptuous, or in one way or another denying the rights and capacities of others.

HOW DO YOU STAND?

The checklist that follows will give you a good indication of whether you have been behaving assertively in your relationships.

_____ My boss, associates, spouse, and friends rarely belittle me or act as though I'm somehow inferior or uninformed. They rarely patronize me or exploit me.

_____ I have no difficulty in pursuing something when I feel strongly that it should be done. For example, if my spouse, children, or family disagree with me about something, I don't hesitate to let them know how I feel.

_____ I don't have any difficulty in saying no to people when I want to say no.

_____ If my spouse or associates are behaving in ways that bother me, I let them know about it straightforwardly without becoming abusive or apologetic.

_____ In work situations, the person or persons I work for know quite clearly what I aspire to; that is, if I want more responsibility, more money, more opportunity, they know it.

_____ If I supervise or provide direction to others (as a parent, manager, teacher, nurse, administrator), people involved know how I feel about work-related issues.

_____ Although people may like me, I am *not* seen as a "pushover" who will cooperate with everybody and is willing to do what others want in order to make them happy.

_____ Although I may be seen as firm and straightforward, people do not find me to be abusive or aggressive.

_____ I often play a key role in making business, family and social decisions, for example, where we should go for dinner, if we should spend more money on new equipment or furniture, how a given problem should be handled.

_____ I rarely end up feeling I should have taken a stronger stand after a disagreement or argument.

_____ I rarely end up feeling that I became nasty and unreasonable after a disagreement.

_____ I'm rarely accused of being hard to understand, longwinded, or evasive.

_____ For the most part I feel I am achieving what I want to achieve based on my capacities, competency, and experience.

If you are able to check most of the previous statements with conviction, then the chances are that you are already behaving assertively in many situations. The balance of this chapter will clarify sources of assertiveness and the differences between assertive and aggressive behavior. It will also indicate ways in which you can increase or continue to channel your energies toward assertive, effective action.

THE SOURCES OF ASSERTIVENESS

By definition assertive behavior is active. It is aimed at influencing events, at expressing your wants, at defending your rights and position. It flows not only from positive feelings, creative drive, energy, ambition and affirmative feelings about yourself and your goals, but is also rooted in feelings that are often described as "negative."

For example, if you shop carefully for an item that is important to you and that you need right away and that item is delivered to your house and is broken, ultimately you will want to behave assertively in order to get the matter straightened out. Your first feeling when you find the desired item broken is probably anger and dissatisfaction. Similarly, if you work and you find you have not received a raise or promotion for which you feel you're qualified, your first feelings are probably somewhat negative. You may be angry with your boss, you may feel the "system" is unfair, you may feel sad or mistreated.

In sports, you may feel a strong competitive urge that sometimes includes anger, tension, or fear. The same kinds of feelings often occur when you are asked to make a public speech or need to discipline someone who has made a mistake or isn't doing a good job. You probably feel some tension or fear by the very nature of the task you've been assigned and you may feel some anger toward some of the people involved. Salespeople, for example, often speak about their customers in "win-lose" terms and with an edge of anger: "I finally got him. He hemmed and hawed for six months and asked for all sorts of information. But I hung in there and refused to let him shove me around. The result is that I finally won the order." Teachers and counselors occasionally feel frustrated and angry with "problem" students or patients. Teachers experience fear quite often when they confront a large group of "undisciplined" students. Thus, negative feelings are quite common and, in fact, they aid you in mobilizing your resources.

Anger, Fear and Assertive Behavior

The most often overlooked sources of assertiveness are fear and anger. You often perform better when you are somewhat tense and when you are in touch with some of your angry feelings as long as you can channel those feelings affirmatively. For example, assume you wish to return damaged merchandise to a department store. Your effectiveness is increased if you are in touch with some of the inconvenience and anger associated with the event. If you approach the store apologetically without conviction or force, you may find that "you lose." On the other hand, if you explode with out-of-control anger, you may encounter someone in the store who explodes back or who becomes uncooperative or quietly surly and resistant. So, a straightforward expression of your feelings, "I am very upset about the damaged merchandise I received and I want my money back" may be much more effective than an enraged acting out of your displeasure. The fact is that if in your dealings with people you are generally straightforward and assertive, the chances of being pushed into a corner where you will have no recourse but to explode with anger and aggression are much less likely. People who demonstrate conviction and strength are rarely pushed around.

Assertive versus Aggressive Behavior

It now becomes possible to clarify further the distinction between aggressive behavior and assertive behavior. Assertive behavior expresses your wants, goals, and feelings. It is straightforward, direct and does *not* put other people down. Though it may include statements of your dissatisfaction, displeasure or anger, it does not deny the rights or individuality of the other person. When you express your wants, goals, or feelings in ways which deny the rights of others you are being aggressive. For example, the clerk to whom you are returning merchandise probably had nothing to do with the fact that the merchandise was damaged. To call the clerk names, attack his/her credibility or reliability, or in one way or another assume that the clerk has no rights or feelings, is aggressive. Thus, any behavior which denies the rights, resources, or dignity of another is aggressive.

You Choose

It's important to recognize that *you* have choices to make. You can choose to be aggressive with the clerk, to vent your anger or displeasure in a very personalized way. This may be the only way you've found to direct your discomfort or irritation. Assertiveness, however, is a positive outlet for these same kinds of feelings. Hence, when you're assertive you express yourself without "dumping" on other people while at the same time making your own purposes clear. Here is a series of examples contrasting assertive and aggressive behavior. See which you think has the best chance of succeeding.

Example 1: Assume you have a subordinate, student, child, or friend who is constantly late for appointments. On the left below you will find an assertive statement dealing with that issue and on the right you will find an aggressive statement. Several examples are given to show the range of possibilities in each area.

Assertive Response	Aggressive Response
You've been late for several appointments. This has caused a great deal of inconvenience for me. I want you to be on time in the future.	I don't know what's the matter with you. You make promises and you never keep them. You're unreliable and I just can't trust you.
I want to talk to you about your lateness and come to an agreement so we can set appointments and be sure they'll be kept.	Well, I guess I'm going to have to treat you like a child and keep reminding you of your responsibilities. I really don't like to have to do that, but evidently you're not mature enough to be on time.
I want to understand if you have problems that are causing you to be late.	I suppose there's something bothering you and that's why you're late. Why don't you grow up?
Your lateness causes quite a few problems for me and for others in the group. There are some disciplinary actions that I plan to take. If you're late again, then you will be (given a warning, sent to the principal's office, "grounded," etc.).	I just won't put up with this kind of behavior. Do this again and you're going to be thrown out of class (sent to bed without supper, lose some of your pay, etc.) because you're just too irresponsible to discipline yourself.

Notice there are often subtle differences between assertive and aggressive statements. Telling someone the negative consequences of a given piece of behavior is assertive. "You are subject to termination if you smoke in a no smoking area." "If you are late for supper again, you won't be permitted to go out for the next three days." These statements may be "tough" but they do not put down the other person and they do not attack him/her in terms of credibility, responsibility, or as a human being. In contrast, statements like, "I won't put up with this any longer, you're irresponsible" are dogmatic and abusive. They are personalized attacks on the individual. They are therefore aggressive.

ASSERTIVENESS GUIDELINES

Following you will find guidelines for assertiveness, things you can do to make your statements and actions increasingly assertive while avoiding inappropriate aggression and unnecessary apologetic or nonassertive behavior.

_____   Express your wants, feelings and ideas straightfor-wardly without apology or putdowns.

_____   Point out the benefits or negative consequences of a given course of action rather than using personal threats or attacks.

_____   Stay in touch with your own feelings and channel those feelings into affirmative actions.

_____   Use positive words and expressions; avoid "loaded" terms and value judgments.

_____   Avoid being petulant, "wish-washy"; don't use a "poor me" approach.

SUMMARY

There is a clear-cut difference between being assertive and being aggressive. Using the examples and checklist provided in this chapter, you can make an initial assessment of your own patterns for getting things done. In later chapters you will have an opportunity to explore and expand upon assertiveness methods and techniques.

Right now there is a second side of the assertiveness coin which is critical to your effectiveness. Not only is it important for you to draw upon your own energies, to push for what you want and to defend yourself against resistance or aggression, it is also important for you to use your resources to tune into and relate to other people, to draw them out and to interact with them effectively. The next chapter deals with this second dimension of "getting things done."

CHAPTER **3**

IT TAKES TWO
AT LEAST

WHATEVER HAPPENED TO
NUMBER TWO?

During the last fifty years Americans have found themselves increasingly subjected to the pressures of an expanding technological and impersonal environment. There is a growing awareness of the danger of "losing your identity." People have begun to feel like numbers—Social Security numbers, employee numbers, license numbers, checking account numbers, credit card numbers. They have also begun to feel that our technology is running us: computers, jet aircraft, electronics and the space age makes us feel inconsequential. A new revolution has been going on during the last several decades to fight against the ever growing pressures to conform to this technological world. Tom Wolfe summed it up by referring to our contemporary interests as representative of the "me generation." Millions of copies of books aimed at making people feel more like individuals, making them more aware of their rights and their individual capacities are indicators of a growing concern with "me." Hundreds of thousands of Americans are attending seminars and training sessions aimed at making them feel more empowered, making it possible for them to concentrate on their own needs and interests, to stand up for their rights and pursue their own goals. One very popular program called Erhard Seminar Training (EST) focuses on the fact that every individual is responsible for his/her own behavior and cannot blame the environment or other people for his/her own problems. This program and various forms of "encounter groups," self-help groups, assertiveness training programs and sessions on "self-realization" and self-awareness are expressions of a deeply felt need among many of us to fight the pressures to conform and the loss of individuality which these pressures bring.

Although many of these endeavors and much of the current paperback literature which surrounds them have been described as "pop" psychology, the fact is the concepts that are being described are rooted in psychological thought and research. The idea that an individual should be clear as to his/her own identity, should essentially "feel good about him/herself," is not a new one. Every major psychologist over the last hundred years has placed a heavy emphasis on the need for every person to feel well-defined and integrated. During more recent years, a school of thought best known as "Gestalt Therapy" has placed even heavier emphasis on the individual's capacity to act on his/her own feelings, to define his/her own goals, and to operate in an autonomous fashion.

ACTION REQUIRES INTERACTION

So much energy and thought has been going into helping people pursue their own goals and rights that there has been a preoccupation with "self." As a result, a second basic ingredient in interpersonal affairs has been overlooked: one cannot act solely on one's own beliefs, needs, and goals without sensitivity to and awareness of the needs and goals of others. It is not possible to survive without interacting with others.

More than that, cooperation and collaboration are an essential part of our contemporary institutions—to development of the family structure, to formation and growth of business endeavors, to establishment and maintenance of the social systems which sustain us: schools, churches, hospitals, and public agencies. It is simply impossible to get anywhere, either in terms of one's own self-interest or in terms of the greater social good, without cooperation. Ambitious, acquisitive business people need mentors, sponsors, loyal subordinates, understanding and aware attorneys and business partners. Energetic, enthusiastic sales representatives increasingly need the cooperation of computer specialists, engineers and technical experts as well as the backing and support of a marketing organization. Schoolteachers can no longer close the door of the classroom and operate autonomously. They are dependent upon collaborative endeavors with educational specialists and often need the support of administrators and parents (and taxpayers).

Regardless of your specific interests, your craft or profession, your social aims and goals, you need other people. However, "need" does not mean that you must lose your identity, become dependent, permit others to define your life or your goals. Need simply means that it is essential for you to draw on other people's resources, to involve them in concerns and projects of interest to you and to the broader society. The capacity to be appropriately interactive is essential if you wish to move forward. Although you may be "number one" in any given situation, you cannot maintain yourself or your position without number two. In fact, it is inevitable in your day-to-day life that you will, in many cases, not be the person "in charge." Managers, Internal Revenue agents, spouses, children, parents, doctors and many others are often more powerful than you are. The fact that another individual knows more or has more resources or experience or more emotional commitment in a given situation does not mean that you must lose your identity or be diminished because of the power and energy of others. It is wise to find ways of relating to that energy, to that power, in order to succeed. Similarly, when you are in a position of power or dominance, it is equally important for you to draw upon the energy and resources of others in order to reach significant objectives.

Basically, when you are the "boss" you need the energy, commitment and support of those around you. When you are the subordinate you need the support, understanding and commitment of your boss. And the same dynamics exist in the teacher-student relationship, the relationship between spouses, siblings, patients and doctors, leaders and followers. In all of these situations each individual has at least one resource which the other cannot replicate. Each individual has his/her own commitment and energy. You cannot force your subordinates, patients, students, children, or spouses to be committed to you or to a project that you favor. You cannot force anyone to utilize his/her fullest range of energies in an activity which that individual does not accept as valid or important.

THE NATURE OF
RESPONSIVENESS

Therefore, human interaction is a two-sided coin. On the opposite side of assertiveness is responsiveness. You are responsive when you tune into, show understanding for, and respect the rights and resources of other people. It is not enough enough to be aware of your own rights and resources, to feel positive about yourself; it is essential, also, to be aware of and responsive to "the other." As is the case with assertive behavior, responsive behavior requires action. People do not know that you are interested, concerned, understanding, empathetic, available unless you show it. People do not know that you want or need their knowledge, their affection, their energy, their influence, unless in some fashion you demonstrate that desire. Responsive behavior is an overt demonstration of your interest and concern for the resources and rights of the other. At times it may be as simple as an expression of curiosity or interest. At other times it may be reflected in a change in your own behavior. For example, if you become aware that your approach to conducting meetings is distracting other people from participating, perhaps frightening them or causing them to withdraw, you then have to reassess your own behavior based on your sensitivity and awareness of what is going on in the group.

Responsiveness is more than simply being aware of the fact that your behavior is causing problems. It may lead you to decide to develop new ways of handling the situation so that others can contribute and participate more effectively. This need not be a denial of your own goals, interests, and personality. Rather, it can be the result of a conscious awareness of what is needed and the development of the capacity to respond to that need effectively and in the best interests of all concerned. If one changes one's mind when faced with new evidence, this is not necessarily a reflection of self-doubt, inadequacy or nonassertive behavior.

Here are some of the ways in which responsiveness is expressed. Note that in none of these instances need you deny your own rights or resources, although in each instance you are not asserting a position. You are responsive if you follow any of the patterns outlined here.

Ask Questions

It is responsive to try to find out what someone else thinks or believes. "How do you feel about this new budget?" Or, "What do you think of this product?" are evidences of a responsive concern for the views of others.

Questions can be used manipulatively in self-serving ways which do not reflect a readiness to listen or to tune in to another's views. Some sales representatives use questions to "entrap" the customer. Some interviewers, teachers, and managers use loaded or leading questions which aim to direct others to a predetermined goal rather than to seek information. A questions such as, "Don't you see how valuable this product could be to you and how much money it would save for you?" is not an attempt to understand the other person's point of view. It is an attempt to lead that person in a given direction. Nor is the teacher who asks, "Don't you think it would be a good idea if you did your homework tonight?" really trying to understand or respond to the homework situation. He/she is simply trying to structure the situation in a predetermined direction.

Thus, questions that are genuinely responsive must reflect your interest in and concern for the views of the other. This does not mean that you will necessarilly respond to the answer affirmatively. For example, a manager may ask a subordinate, "I've been thinking about ways of cutting costs in this department. Do you have some suggestions as to things we might do?" The question does not mean that the manager is going to adopt the subordinate's suggestions. It means that there is an interest in getting the subordinate's ideas.

Note, too, that responsiveness is not always compassionate and affectionate. You may ask questions to try to understand and respond to the other person's position even though you don't support or like that position. For example, a doctor might say to a patient, "I don't understand why you won't stop smoking. Can you explain to me why you haven't quit?" As long as the question is a genuine search for information, not a manipulation to force the other person into a predetermined position, then one is behaving responsively.

Accept Differences

When you are confronted with resistance or disagreement, one of the strongest temptations is to attack that resistance or disagreement. It is tempting to point out the flaws in another's argument, to "talk" him/her out of objections, to use persuasion to try to swing the person to your point of view. There are many instances when these assertive and perhaps even aggressive modes of behavior may produce results. However, often the best way to overcome resistance and to deal with complex problems is to show understanding of the other person's point of view. This does not mean you necessarily agree with that person or plan to act in accordance with his/her wishes. It simply means that you try to understand "where that person is coming from."

For example, a dissatisfied customer returns a piece of merchandise and says to the clerk, "I don't know how you can sell junk like this. It fell apart before I got a chance to use it." The clerk may be tempted to "fight back" and say something like, "Well, I've sold hundreds of these and this is the first time I've had a complaint," or, "I use one of these myself and I can tell you that it works fine." It is conceivable that the customer would back off if given this kind of information. However, most of us have learned from experience that that's not the most likely action. More often than not the customer comes back more combatively and says something like, "I don't care how many of these you've sold. It's still a piece of junk," or, "Don't tell me about your experience with this. I just finished trying to make it work and it's a mess." And from that point on the fight may escalate.

In contrast, the responsive mode, which accepts differences without implying agreement, is to reflect back that you have heard what has been said, to show empathy or concern for the position of the other. A statement like, "I can see you're upset. Tell me more about what happened" is responsive and, also, it is neutral. You are neither admitting to a flaw in the product nor are you putting pressure on the other person to change his/her view. After the facts have been discussed, and the person has a chance to express his/her views, then you may wish to become more assertive and take a firm position on the issue.

Here is a short dialogue between a parent and a child showing how the responsive mode works (right-hand column) and, in contrast, how a more combative "me first" approach affects the situation.

Here is a second example showing the use of questions and other responsive modes which produces clear and positive benefits.

Change Your Mind

One of the common misconceptions regarding influence and power is that powerful people don't change their minds. They are firm, intractable, and unchanging. However, when one begins examining truly critical issues well handled by success-ful leaders, it becomes clear that many effective leaders are not fixed and unyielding. They are often responsive to the views of others, to changing information and circumstances.

When Dwight D. Eisenhower was the commanding gen-eral responsible for the invasion of continental Europe, he appraised and reappraised the changing circumstances. He studied troop movements, received periodic weather reports, consulted with various experts, and from time to time seemed to favor delay in the landings on the French coast. When the point of decision came, he decided firmly what should be done, but only after showing much potential for change. John F. Kennedy behaved similarly when dealing with the Cuban missile crisis: the Soviet Union was transporting missiles into Cuba and a decision to act had to be made. In the process of deciding this issue a group of advisors gathered and dis-cussed the problem over an extended period of time. Various alternatives were selected, Kennedy listened, asked questions, and left the group alone from time to time. Clearly, he did not have a fixed position; he was not sure as to the next step. Finally, after a great deal of problem solving and much chang-ing of positions among all of the persons involved, it was de-

Unresponsive Behavior	*Responsive Behavior*
Child: My teacher is a jerk.	Child: My teacher is a jerk.
Parent: Don't you think you'd have a better chance of getting along if you didn't think that way?	Parent: I'd like to understand why you feel that way. What's been happening in school?
Child: I can't help it if the teacher is a jerk. He just behaves foolishly. It isn't fair.	Child: Well, the teacher just keeps talking and never gives me a chance to talk. The other kids don't like him either.
Parent: Now you have to understand that there are thirty-five other children in your class and I'm sure the teacher has a lot on his mind. It isn't right for you to talk about him that way.	Parent: I see. You'd like a chance to talk more in class.
Child: Why do you always take the teacher's side? You never understand my side. I still think he's a jerk no matter what you say.	Child: Well, it isn't so much that I'd like to talk more. It's just that I don't understand why the teacher talks so much.
	Parent: What do you think the teacher is trying to do when he's talking?
	Child: I don't know. I guess partly he's trying to show off and show us how smart he is, but I guess he also wants us to know more.
	Parent: Well, how do you feel about that?
	Child: I guess I do want to know more, but it's difficult to learn from this guy.
Outcome: Perhaps the child stamps out of the room. Perhaps the adult administers discipline. Perhaps they simply stop talking. In any case, as things are going, resolution is unlikely.	*Outcome:* The world does not change based on a brief conversation. The child may still be impatient and uncomfortable with the teacher. However, he/she is not alienated from the parent. They can continue to discuss the problem. They can begin to examine some alternative ways to deal with it.

Unresponsive Behavior

Responsive Behavior

Customer: I'd like to buy this product but I just don't have the money.

Sales Rep: Well, of course, everybody says that but you know you can scrape the money together if you really want to. I notice that you smoke. If you gave up just one pack a day, you'll be able to pay off the cost of this item pretty quickly.

Customer: Well, to tell you the truth, I've tried to give up smoking and I really don't want to. You may think I can scrape up the money but, believe me, I'm just short of cash.

Sales Rep: Well, maybe we can work out a time payment plan that you could handle. For example, could you pay $12 a month?

Customer: Look, I know about these time payment plans. I don't want to get myself in any deeper. Let's just forget it.

Outcome: If the sales representative keeps pushing and selling, there's a good chance that he/she won't break through the resistance. In the first place, he/she doesn't know what the real problem is. In the second place, there's been little progress toward mutual understanding. Of course, the sale is still possible, but the resistance hasn't really been dealt with and makes the sale less likely.

Customer: I'd like to buy this product but I just don't have the money.

Sales Rep: I see. You do feel that this product would suit your needs. The difficulty is getting the money together to pay for it.

Customer: Yes, if I could find some way to pay for it I'd buy it.

Sales Rep: Well, there are a couple of options for covering the cost. First, let's calculate what savings the product will bring you. That's about $12 a month. You could make weekly or monthly payments. Which do you prefer?

Outcome: Notice that the sales representative has not "fought" the customer's objections. Rather, he/she has begun to show ways in which those objections can be dealt with, perhaps by computing the savings and prorating them and developing a time payment plan. Assuming that the customer truly wants the product, the probable outcome is that the customer and the sales representative can work out a solution if the exchange stays in this problem-solving vein. It has not become a "win-lose" contest.

cided that a blockade was the best decision. Fortunately for world peace the strategy worked, whereas a more hard-line position, which Kennedy might well have taken early in the discussions, could have been extremely damaging.

Note, then, that it is not enough in interpersonal affairs simply to be assertive, to take a position, to sell your ideas, to quietly maintain or vigorously espouse a given cause or concern. It is often necessary to seek information from others and to alter your viewpoint based on new facts and new insights in an effort to obtain a greater contribution or commitment from those around you. In complex social and management situations there is rarely a "right" answer. Rather, there's a suitable course of action which will generate support and interest. There's an answer that people can support, work with, and pursue. Often one cannot think in terms of the absolute best way in a technical or statistical sense. One must think in terms of the totality of the situation. One must be responsive to the feelings, reactions, and behavior of others.

Responsiveness which involves changing one's mind is neither nonassertive nor manipulative when it is representative of a genuine openness to new ideas, to divergent feelings and to the realities of a complex social situation. A good example of the responsive mode occurred when an engineering staff was asked to determine the "best" way to assemble a radio. From a technical and engineering point of view, the "best" way to do the job was to break it down into parts, to assign each worker a portion of the assembly, to set up an assembly line, and to have everyone follow the procedure precisely. However, when the issue was discussed with employees, it became clear that they wanted to do more than simply insert one or two parts into a chassis passing before them on an assembly line belt. They wanted to build the radios themselves. As a result, the managers decided that the "best" way needed to be tempered by other elements in the situation: the feelings and attitudes of people, their drives, capacities, and interests. The robot-like assembly line was not installed and a more involving and humanized system was introduced.

Production in the new system turned out to be significantly better than in the past and better than competitors who were using a more routinized approach, all the result of management's responsiveness. Note, also, that this responsiveness did not deny what the managers and engineers knew, but made possible the utilization of the ideas and interests of everyone. Nor did management weaken its authority by getting ideas from the workers.

SEEKING AFFECTION—
AVOIDING GUILT

Responsiveness, however, can slip into behavior that is not directed at truly responding to the needs and goals of the other person nor integrated with your own concerns and best interests. If you are more concerned with having other people like you than you are with getting a job done or reaching a goal, there's a good chance that you will achieve neither. For example, a well-known study in industry showed that supervisors who were deeply concerned with being liked were less effective in getting the job done and had lower morale among the workers than other supervisors who were more concerned with working with people to achieve results. Most of us know people who are so eager to win our affection and esteem that they are not straightforward. They continually try to please us and end up by not being our best friends. The chances are that your best friends are people who are interested enough in you to be straightforward, to take the risk of disagreeing with you, or to point out when they feel you are wrong. A friend, then, is often someone who will take the risk of giving you "negative feedback." Therefore, it is important not to confuse the need to be liked with the capacity and need to be responsive.

Responsiveness occurs when you are interested and concerned with the other person's point of view but have not lost touch with your own goals, needs, and interests. If your major objective in a relationship is to have the other person like you, then you may gradually become so accommodating, wishy-washy, or deferential that you won't attract the other person's interest or win his/her affection.

Similarly, if your motivation in working with people is to avoid or cope with your own feelings of guilt, you may react in ways that are not straightforward and genuinely responsive, ways that are, in fact, harmful. For example, assume you have someone who works with you in a somewhat subordinate position (a direct subordinate in business, a student, a younger and somewhat dependent friend) and you have been very busy and haven't spent as much time as you would have liked helping that person on a specific activity or project for which he/she is responsible. The time has come when the person should be removed from the activity because of inadequate performance. You may feel uncomfortable or guilty because you haven't done much to help this person. This guilty feeling may cause you to hesitate to be genuinely assertive and responsive in dealing with that person, so you may try to be a "nice person" and soften the criticism so that the individual fails to get the message. If the individual asks for another chance, you may delay the removal and rationalize that you are being responsive. Yet you know that the individual is not performing to the level desired and that by permitting him/her to continue in that position you may be denying others an opportunity and impairing performance. Also, the individual involved may begin to feel uncomfortable about his/her level of performance and may become less mature in coping with his/her own responsibilities. Softness or responses based on guilt are not truly responsive. They are not a reflection of your true concern with the other person's competency, rights and resources, nor are they a reflection of your own awareness of what's really going on.

If you feel guilty or have a great need for another person's affection or esteem, it is important to face up to that feeling and to deal with it straightforwardly within yourself. For example, a manager might say to a subordinate: "It certainly would have been beneficial if you and I had spent more time together during the period when you were learning the job; however, that was not possible. As it stands now you are not performing up to what the job demands or, probably, up to your capacity; therefore, it's necessary for me to transfer you off the job." In dealing with a friend it may be appropriate to say, "I'm very fond of you. I want whatever I do to be in your best interests. I'm convinced that if you continue in your present role (whether it's a member of the Little League team or vice-president of a corporation), you will not be serving the best interests of the organization (team). In fact, until you take steps to improve your own performance, you'll not operate at the level at which I know you're capable." Given this assertive stance (without guilt, without apology, without an undue need to retain the other person's affection at any cost) it is then possible to be responsive: "I realize this change may be upsetting to you and I want to work it out in a way that will be in both of our long-term best interests. I would suggest a temporary transfer. Tell me how you feel about that."

In such a situation the other individual may disagree, may come back combatively, or may simply try to talk you out of your position. The basic assertive-responsive mode, treating the issue as a shared problem, will serve well to work through this issue.

In summary, the major thrust of the examples that have been given is that the essence of responsiveness comes from an awareness of what's really going on in the situation. Thus, you listen not simply to be polite or to show affection or understanding. You listen in order to learn more about the situation, to be able to tune in and respond to what's going on. You modify, adapt, or adjust your own behavior not to satisfy the other person or to make him/her feel better but to develop a more effective course of action, one that will be in the long-term best interests of those involved—including yourself.

Responsiveness is neither humble nor heroic. It is a communication pattern; it is a mode of reacting to people which can improve your capacity to get things done and to fulfill your own purposes as well as to facilitate the accomplishment and success of those with whom you are involved.

HOW DO YOU STAND?

The brief checklist which follows will give you a good indication of whether you have been behaving responsively in your relationships with the people with whom you are involved.

_____   I am able to listen to people without feeling that I am being a "pushover" or manipulating them.

_____   I find it's useful to learn how other people feel.

_____   When people disagree with me, my first act or reaction is *not* to disagree in return or to point out the flaws in their argument.

_____   Although people know that I'll listen to their point of view and that I will change my mind, they know it will only be when I'm convinced that the new position is appropriate.

_____   I don't have any difficulty in admitting to myself that I've made a mistake nor in accepting information

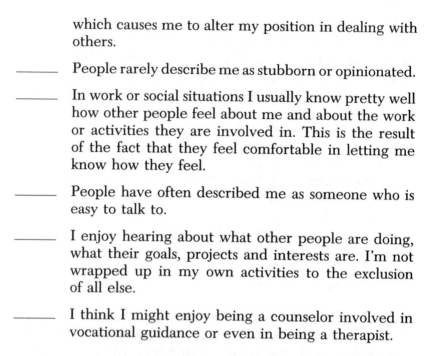

which causes me to alter my position in dealing with others.

_____ People rarely describe me as stubborn or opinionated.

_____ In work or social situations I usually know pretty well how other people feel about me and about the work or activities they are involved in. This is the result of the fact that they feel comfortable in letting me know how they feel.

_____ People have often described me as someone who is easy to talk to.

_____ I enjoy hearing about what other people are doing, what their goals, projects and interests are. I'm not wrapped up in my own activities to the exclusion of all else.

_____ I think I might enjoy being a counselor involved in vocational guidance or even in being a therapist.

If you were able to check most of the statements or this checklist, the chances are good that you are often responsive in dealing with other people. However, there is a subtle problem as one moves towards the more responsive mode.

THE "NICE GUY" SYNDROME

Strangely, a great many people who move into what have been called the "helping" professions are seen by those who work with them as anything but helpful. For example, when teachers have been asked why they chose the teaching profession, many said, "I enjoy working with children" or, "I like helping people." Many of these same teachers are seen by their students as being rigid, intolerant, or condescending and contemptuous. Several studies of psychotherapists have shown that quite a few therapists use their positions to manipulate people and to satisfy their own needs for power; they enjoy quietly and subtly pulling strings and playing on the emotions of others. Many persons with a great deal of experience in personnel work make the point that the individual interested in the personnel field who says "I want to be in Personnel because I like people" is probably not going to be a good personnel specialist. Clearly, these are generalizations and certainly do not apply across the board.

Nevertheless, "liking people" is often a cover-up for one's own inability to compete actively in the real world, and it is often an expression of withheld aggression. Many of us have learned through bitter experience that the individual who seems constantly to be self-effacing, humble, loving and concerned is nonetheless capable of a great deal of hostility and bitterness. Aggression and anger are normal human feelings that should and do crop up frequently on a day-to-day basis. Therefore, when one suppresses the natural aggression and hostility that's bound to occur in the contemporary world, and covers it over with a soft shell of sweetness, in many instances it remains bottled up and either explodes dramatically or seeps out in subtle and destructive ways.

Most children, for example, would rather deal with a parent or teacher who occasionally blows up with anger than one who is always sweet and gentle but nevertheless administers dehumanizing punishment. Thus, it is probably better to become angry with a child than to quietly and calmly close him/her off in a dark room for three or four hours or to ostracize the child. The first punishment may be administered aggressively, the second may be done in a gentle and sweet way: "I don't like to do this to you but after all, you've been a bad boy and it's important for you to learn how to behave, so you're going to have to spend the next two hours in the cloakroom." The social isolation and fear of being locked in a cloakroom is much more punitive than an explosive verbal outburst. The point is that even if you were able to check all the items on the previous list, it is still important to recognize that unless your ability to be responsive is coupled with the ability to be assertive and unless you are in touch with your own anger and aggression, then the responsive mode may simply be a cover-up for your own hostile feelings. It is important, therefore, to recognize that a second checklist should be considered before you rate yourself as an open, responsive person.

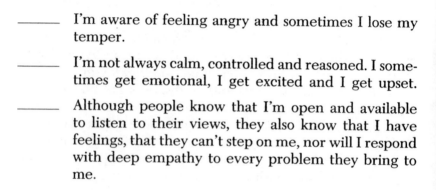

_____ I'm aware of feeling angry and sometimes I lose my temper.

_____ I'm not always calm, controlled and reasoned. I sometimes get emotional, I get excited and I get upset.

_____ Although people know that I'm open and available to listen to their views, they also know that I have feelings, that they can't step on me, nor will I respond with deep empathy to every problem they bring to me.

If you were able to check the last three items as well as most of the items in the previous list, then you can feel assured as to your genuine responsiveness. If, on the other hand, you respond to other people in a helpful, constructive, and supportive way in part because you don't want to take the chance of expressing your own feelings, or admitting to your own anger, fear or boredom, then it may be that you use responsiveness in a manipulative way—a way which gives you a feeling of power and control in the situation without taking a great deal of personal risk.

Put in very simple terms, talking without listening is ineffective. Conversely, listening without talking is ineffective. Although you may listen for periods of time, and contain your own feelings in given situations, your own emotionality needs to be available to you if you want to optimize your effectiveness and develop genuine trust and rapport with others.

THE SOURCES OF RESPONSIVENESS

Why are we responsive? In part because we are concerned about others. Most of us are willing to suffer discomfort, at times, in order to bring more comfort and pleasure to our children, parents, or siblings. Our concerns extend outside the family because we live in a world of interdependencies. We are continuously building relationships through which we can achieve shared goals—groups, clans, tribes, teams, organizations, and societies. And our interdependencies move us to seek recognition and acceptance. So our responsiveness flows from concerns for self as well as for others.

RESPONSIVE VERSUS NONASSERTIVE BEHAVIOR

In Chapter 2, a clear-cut distinction was made between aggressive behavior and assertive behavior. Assertive behavior expresses your wants, goals, and feelings without putting people down; aggressive behavior contains put-downs. A similar distinction can now be made between responsive and nonassertive behavior. You are responsive when you show concern for the goals, wants, and rights of other people without denying your own. When you act in ways which diminish or fail to protect your rights or interests, you are being nonassertive. Here are a few examples to make the distinction clear.

Assume you disagree with someone regarding the solution to a problem. However, you want to show a willingness

to consider the other person's point of view and to be responsive to his/her needs, interests, and rights. Here are some
responsive ways of interacting in that situation.

> *"I'd like to know more about your point of view."*
>
> *"I favor course of action A; however, I'd like to hear more
> about your approach (which is different from mine)." (Note
> that this statement contains an assertion coupled with a show
> of concern and interest.)*
>
> *"I gather you feel course of action B would work best." (Note
> here that the individual simply shows that he/she understands
> the other person's point of view and leaves the situation open
> for further discussion.)*

In contrast, here are some possible nonassertive responses
to the same situation.

> *"I'm awfully sorry that we can't agree on this. I guess I've
> been stubborn and unreasonable. Please bear with me."*
>
> *"I know you have a lot more experience in these things than
> I do and I hope you will try to understand my position. I
> think if you'll help me out I can get the job done properly."*
>
> *"I understand how you can get this done in the way you've
> suggested, but you've got to remember that I'm not as skillful
> in these things as you are. I may have to follow a different
> course of action because I'm just not able to be as effective
> as you."*

The second set of statements is apologetic and self-demeaning; they involve self put-downs. It is never necessary
to deny your own rights, interests, or feelings in order to show
understanding or concern for the feelings of another. Even
in instances when you choose to follow a course of action
which is not ideal, it is still not necessary to be nonassertive
in your reactions. For example, assume that someone in higher

authority wants you to do a job differently than you feel it should be done. After examining the situation you recognize that the other person's approach may not be what you want but it is an alternate way of doing the job. It does not violate your beliefs, your ethics, or your responsibilities. Therefore, you might respond with a statement which contains both assertive and responsive elements such as, "I understand the way you want this done and your reasons for it. I feel the alternative I suggested would work more effectively. However, I know I can make the approach you suggest work. I think it's important we move forward on a basis that we both see as having a good chance of success."

RESPONSIVENESS GUIDELINES

Given the background and nature of responsibilities here are some guidelines to aid you in developing the responsive modes of interaction.

_____ In striving to solve a problem, seek out the opinions and experience of the other person.

_____ Even when you disagree with another, be sure you understand his/her point of view and the reasoning behind it before pursuing a course of action.

_____ Keep in mind that commitment to a course of action is often as important as the course of action itself. For example, in a team situation it is often necessary for individuals to be responsive and adaptive in order to develop an approach which can be supported by everyone.

_____ In showing understanding and concern for the other, avoid apologies, self-demeaning statements, and self put-downs.

———— In any discussion in which there is disagreement, keep exploring the other person's point of view. As progress is made, test for "acceptance" by asking questions and summarizing what has been agreed to.

———— Recognize and demonstrate that changing your mind or modifying your position when faced with new information is an effective problem-solving response.

ASSERTIVENESS PLUS RESPONSIVENESS EQUALS ACTION

It is often necessary to utilize your own resources and the resources of others to get things done. As indicated earlier, assertiveness and responsiveness are not different behaviors. Rather, they are components of an open, problem-solving approach to other people and to the issues you share. The ways in which the modes can be combined will be discussed in the chapters which follow. First, a design or model for improvement will be provided.

CHAPTER **4**

GETTING THERE

A MODEL

To improve in almost any endeavor, it is often essential to have a picture in your mind of how that endeavor looks when it's being done well. For example, if you want to improve your golf swing, you need to have an image of what a good swing looks like. Without that image, you will simply swing the club in a random way and it will take quite a while to discover an appropriate approach to the swing. On the other hand, if you've seen other people play golf, and you've been shown the "right way," then you may find an effective swing much more rapidly. If you want to be a more effective public speaker, sales representative, dancer, or truck driver, it is essential to develop positive images of how each one functions. The driver of an 18-wheel tractor-trailer needs to have a picture in his/her mind of what happens to the trailer when it is being backed into a narrow space properly. A surgeon needs a picture of various operating procedures to perform them well.

In these and dozens of other instances the first time a given task is performed it is usually performed against a model. If you think of the first time you bowled or sewed a button on a piece of fabric or performed a technical operation, the chances are someone "showed you how to do it"—they provided you with a model, a procedure, or an approach to performing the task.

This approach to learning is taken for granted and practiced in almost every area. In some fields the use of models or systematic procedures is a carefully defined part of the learning process. A surgeon is not permitted to practice surgery professionally until he/she has been provided with specific procedures and models and tried them out in practice situations. A lawyer practices law in a "mock" courtroom before being admitted to the bar. The lawyer watches other trained professionals, uses them as models; he/she carefully and intensively studies model court cases and trial procedures.

In almost any field where high levels of performance are essential, ideal models are presented and practiced and very little is left to chance. Strangely, the rigorous effort that goes into becoming a lawyer or a ballet dancer is *not* exercised in learning how to become a more effective manager or a more effective parent or a more socially aware and adept individual.

In the next several chapters you will be provided with brief models of ways in which you can behave in order to interact with others more effectively. As is the case in any activity requiring great skill, it is not enough to know the model or to practice it one or two times. Ultimately the dancer must get on the stage, the lawyer must get into the courtroom. They must try out new behavior and get feedback and try again. Exercise and practice are part of any significant learning experience. Therefore, as you go through the models, various exercises and drills will be suggested and, above all, you are urged to use the resources you find in your environment (teachers, friends, supervisors, subordinates, family members) to work with you in designing a plan for improvement.

ASSERTIVENESS AND RESPONSIVENESS: A PLANNING MODEL

1. Set goals
2. Develop a pathway to your goals
3. Know the rules/techniques for getting there
4. Identify and apply your resources

Each of these four steps is essential to achievement in any field of endeavor. Each step will be described and you will have a chance to think it through and determine how you choose to implement that step.

SET GOALS

The first step in moving toward the achievement of your goals is to know what you want. When people are asked what they want—as you may recall from completing the checklist in Chapter 1—it's easy for most of them to identify broad or general needs and goals: "I want a better job," "I want success," or, "I want happiness" are common first reactions. However, there are four important components to this part of the model for assertiveness.

1. Your chances of achieving your goals are increased dramatically when you make your goals *specific.*
2. Your chances of getting what you want increase if your goals are *measurable.*
3. Your ability to move toward what you want is enhanced when you have a *timetable.*
4. Knowing what you want is of little value if the goals are so far removed, so unreal, so unrelated to the people around you that there's no chance of achieving them. Therefore, the fourth element in moving toward achievement is to identify goals and opportunities which are feasible or *"doable."*

These four elements of goals and plans—make goals specific and measurable, have a timetable and make goals "doable"—are interrelated. Here are some examples to illustrate how these four steps can be carried out.

Make Goals Specific

For a goal to be specific you must be able to describe it graphically and accurately, in a way that leaves no doubt as to its nature. For example, a goal such as "I want to be more successful" is useful in a general way but does not move you towards action until it is translated into more specific terms. One of the ways that this idea has been expressed in business and management situations is "A goal or objective is a statement of a condition that will exist in the future." Accordingly, in connection with success, there may be quite a few conditions that you want to exist in the future such as, "I want to have a management position in the organization" or "I want to own my own business" or "I want to earn 20 percent more than I'm earning now." If you are able to express your goals in specific terms, it is more probable that you will direct your energy towards achievement and be assertive. For example, the feelings associated with the broad statement "I want to get to know more people" versus the statement "Tomorrow while I'm at work I'm going to talk to Mary Smith and find out more about what she's interested in," are quite different.

When you approach another person with a specific objective, when you have decided you want to know more about that person, you will be in a better position to combine assertiveness with responsiveness.

Make Goals Measurable

In the process of becoming more specific, you are making your goals more measurable. Rather than saying, "I want to make more friends" you are now saying, "I'm going to meet

two people this week and I plan to do the following . . ."
Similarly, rather than saying, "I want to make more money,"
make your goal more specific as, "I want to increase my income 10 percent in the next three months." The second goal
is measurable; the first is not. The second goal provides you
with a clear target.

Have a Timetable

As you become specific and make your goals measurable, they
tend to fall into a time frame. If not, it's important to establish
time goals. A statement like "I want to learn more about job
opportunities in my field" is abstract and not sufficiently specific. It is not measurable and there is no time frame. As you
bring it into sharper focus, it begins to sound more like this:
"I'm going to visit three shops (factories, businesses, etc.) like
my own *this week* to find out exactly what opportunities exist."

Make Goals "Doable"

By making your goals specific and measurable and by putting
them in a time frame, the chances are the goals will become
more "doable." A broad, nonspecific goal like "becoming more
fulfilled" is not anywhere near as achievable as a specific, measurable goal with a target date such as "I'm going to join
the bowling team (chess club, great books discussion group,
etc.) next week." Or, "I'm going to go to the theater twice
next month" or "invite two of my co-workers over for dinner
next Saturday." Almost any goal, regardless of its immensity,
can be cut down to size by simply looking for parts of it that
are "doable." For example, running for the state senate is a
rather difficult and long-term objective. However, that objective can be converted into "doable" things by identifying specific subgoals or steps: "I'm going to join the Democratic or
Republican Club this week." If you join the club you might

then set other specific subgoals—"I'm going to take part in the next political campaign," or "I'm going to learn what I have to do to obtain an office in the club."

Knowing what you want is a critical ingredient in becoming more assertive and in moving towards achievement. In most instances, you must also consider other people to make your goals "doable." So, if you want a promotion, it is important to plan not only the specific, measurable, "doable" steps and when they can be taken, it is equally important to be aware of and responsive to your boss's needs and expectations.

There is no way of getting from where you are to where you want to be without taking one step at a time. The critical ingredient in planning for achievement is to identify the steps that need to be taken. The only way to start is to know where you're going and with whom you need to interact to achieve results.

DEVELOP A PATHWAY
TO YOUR GOALS

In large measure the very act of clarifying what you want and setting specific, measurable, "doable" targets begins to define a pathway, a direction to follow. The critical ingredient in further developing a pathway to your goal is to clarify the relationship between what you want to achieve (your end) and how you plan to achieve it (your means). Assume, for example, that you're interested in golf and you want to improve your game. Your goal is to reduce the number of strokes you have to take (the number of times you have to hit the ball) to get from the beginning to the end of the course. Your goal can be expressed specifically and measurably and with a timetable; it can be expressed in "doable" terms. "I want to cut five strokes off my game by the end of the summer." If you set your goals unrealistically high ("I want to develop from a mediocre amateur to a professional golfer in the next three months"), there is very little you can do to move toward that goal without becoming frustrated. However, you may set a long-term goal such as "I want to be a professional golfer" and convert this into short-term actions like "I will take five strokes off my game this summer." Even this goal can be planned more specifically: "This week I will take one stroke off my game."

Nevertheless, all of these goals or desires are targets. They are things you want to achieve. In order to achieve them you must do something. There must be a "how to" or means to your end. So you begin by asking yourself the question, "How do I cut strokes off my game?" and you come up with at least two or three answers. "I can cut the strokes off my game by improving my drive (my long shots)." Or, "I can cut strokes off my game by improving my putting (the short strokes near the hole)." Any or all of these specific goals can be worked on, can be practiced. You can go to the golf range and practice your long shots. You can go to the putting green and practice your short strokes. You can get instruction or advice so as to get rid of bad habits (hooking or slicing the ball, etc.). Depending on how important the goal is to you, you determine how many actions you wish to take and how much energy you want to invest. The point is that you will improve if you are clear, specific, and committed about "how to" proceed.

Means and Ends

This process applies to any activity in which you're involved. You can reduce that activity to a pathway with "doable" steps. One of the ways to establish such a pathway toward your goal involves a technique called Means-Ends Analysis. Very simply, this technique clarifies the "how to's," the means that you have available in order to achieve your purpose or end.

For example, assume you would like to become a leader in some activity or in the community. One action you might take is to learn more about your field of interest. By again asking "how?" you can reduce that item to an even more specific and "doable" activity, for example, attend a special course, read a book, get involved in a project, or talk to a specialist. As indicated in an earlier chapter, if you want something from somebody it may be appropriate simply to identify your interests such as "I want more leadership responsibility. What do I need to do to get it?" This question could be addressed to your immediate supervisor or to a personnel director, or it might be modified somewhat and addressed to the mayor of your town or to a community leader.

The important thing to remember in thinking through your goals and translating them into more specific steps is to ask the question, "How do I get to where I want to go?" Or, expressing it another way, "What do I have to do in order to achieve my goal?" You will become increasingly specific as you continue to raise the question "how?"

There are usually several pathways to a given goal, although one may be better than another. Therefore, it is useful at every step of the analysis to ask the question, "How else might I achieve this goal or end?" For example, suppose your goal is: "I want to get promoted." One means or "how?" might be to strengthen your leadership abilities. That alternative can be analyzed further and specific action steps can be pinned down. However, before proceeding with that analysis, it is useful to consider other alternatives by asking, "How else might I get promoted?" Other options might occur such as "by looking for a job at another company," "by getting more visibility," or "by increasing my versatility." Each of these alternatives, and many others, can then be analyzed and pushed down the Means-Ends chain by repeatedly asking the question "How?"

Note that any possible action step can be related to its higher level goal simply by asking the question "why?" "Why do I want to get more visibility in my job?" Answer: "To get a raise" or "to win recognition and job satisfaction." So this technique of analysis involves "Hows?" and "Whys?" Hence, it's called Means-Ends Analysis.

As you think through issues in this way and make specific plans, you are developing a pathway toward your goal. By converting long-term, relatively vague goals into specific, measurable actions you are isolating alternatives so that if one pathway doesn't work you are not completely blocked. Just as the case with the professional golfer, you may be working on several parts of your "game plan" simultaneously. So you may be attending special classes to learn more about your field of interest, you may also be developing specific plans to get to know more people in your field of activity. You may be working on a relationship with your boss by asking questions and working with him/her to set goals and make plans. You may also be visiting other companies or schools or talking to personnel specialists or consultants to provide other avenues for your own development and growth.

At the end of this chapter a sample Means-Ends Analysis is shown. It indicates how one individual developed several pathways to become more assertive. You will have an opportunity to work out a similar plan for achieving one of your goals.

Keep Your Options Open

In planning for achievement many individuals put all their eggs in one basket. For example, the teacher who wants to get ahead in his/her field may put all of his/her energy into taking courses based on the assumption that "when I have my master's degree or Ph.D. I will be promoted" or "I will be more effective" or "I will be more satisfied." These conclusions are not necessarily true. It may be that promotion requires more than obtaining additional credits. It may require that you get to know more about administrative procedures within the school or university. It may mean you have to expand your contacts both in the school and in your profession.

The same kind of thinking applies to many areas of activity. It is dangerous to assume that any single action or achievement will be enough to propel you to your goal. It is important, therefore, to consider several possible courses of action and possibly pursue two or more simultaneously.

KNOW THE RULES/
TECHNIQUES FOR GETTING
THERE

In every field there is a body of knowledge which can be studied and understood in order to improve one's chances of achieving results. For example, if you want to get ahead in business, it may be necessary for you to learn more about selling, finance, or general management. If you want to improve your effectiveness in interacting with people, there's information on motivation and listening techniques which can help you. If you want to be a better musician, there's no question but that you're going to have to learn and practice the techniques of your craft. For most of those who want to be more effective in selling their ideas, it's necessary to learn more about the selling process. In other words, there are rules, procedures, techniques, and models of behavior which relate to each area of activity. Most people who want to improve their proficiency have to learn about the body of knowledge in their chosen field. This applies equally to those who want to become more assertive. Indeed, as the sample Means-Ends Analysis appearing at the end of this chapter indicates, learning the techniques of assertiveness is one of several important actions that a person can take to become more assertive even though by itself this will probably not be sufficient.

IDENTIFY AND APPLY YOUR RESOURCES

Very often in striving toward achievement of personal goals, individuals assume they must change the core of themselves. For example, one who aspires to a higher-level management position may work under the assumption that "I am quiet, soft-spoken, and rarely lose my temper. I've got to become loud and aggressive in order to get ahead." Yet if one looks around top management one finds successful people who are soft-spoken and rarely lose their temper; they have learned to move out on their feelings constructively, to integrate their reasons and emotions in order to achieve the results they want.

It may not be appropriate for you to be more explosive. You may have to find ways of directing your quiet, controlled approach into increasingly effective outcomes. That does not mean you shouldn't strive to be more outgoing. It means that the key to success for most people is learning to use what they have to full advantage. The goal, then, is not to change yourself in any fundamental way, but to utilize and direct your energies constructively and to your own advantage. This may result in what appears to be change, but for many people it simply means that they're using latent abilities that up to then have been untapped. Here are some of the ways in which you can identify your resources.

1. Review your past experience. What have you done well? What have you felt good about?
2. Obtain guidance or feedback from others: counselors, teachers, friends, or senior business associates.
3. Experiment with new behavior and new information: take

courses, try a new assignment, read in fields of interest, and try out new behavior.

ASSERTIVE-RESPONSIVE
BEHAVIOR AND ACHIEVEMENT

All of the steps covered in this chapter are designed to aid you in planning for achievement.

- ☐ Set Goals
- ☐ Develop a Pathway Toward Your Goals
- ☐ Know the Rules/Techniques for Getting There
- ☐ Identify and Apply Your Resources

Each of the steps in this planning-for-achievement model contributes to your capacity to interact with others assertively and responsively. When you "know where you're going" you come across with assurance. When you have step-by-step plans you have a framework for taking action. When you know what you do well—when you feel good about yourself—you are able to interact with confidence and resilience.

The Means-Ends analysis illustrated on the next page will aid you in planning for achievement. Use it to chart the steps you can take to achieve one of your goals.

HOW TO CONSTRUCT
A MEANS-ENDS ANALYSIS

1. Identify a want or goal.
2. Ask "How can I achieve the goal?" (What do I need to do?)
3. Ask "How else might I achieve this goal?"
4. Keep asking "How?" until you get to "doable" things.
5. Be prepared, in important goals, to do more than one thing. That is, you can pursue several pathways simultaneously.

Here's an example showing how to construct a Means-Ends chart. First, write a brief statement of your goal near the top-middle of a sheet of paper. Place a box around your goal (see below).

Next, ask "How?" and place a box below the first box. Then ask, "How else?" and place a box next to the one you just completed. This procedure is demonstrated in regard to the goal: "I want to be more assertive." After starting the goal, several "How?" boxes are filled in.

Note, more items might be added across the page by continuing to ask "How else might I be more assertive?" Next, continue exploring for "doable" things or means to your end by asking "How?" on each item. Place answers in boxes as shown below.

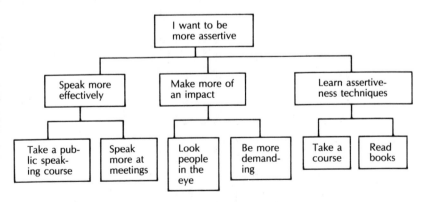

Again, more items can be added by asking "How else?" Each of these items can be reduced to "doable" steps. For

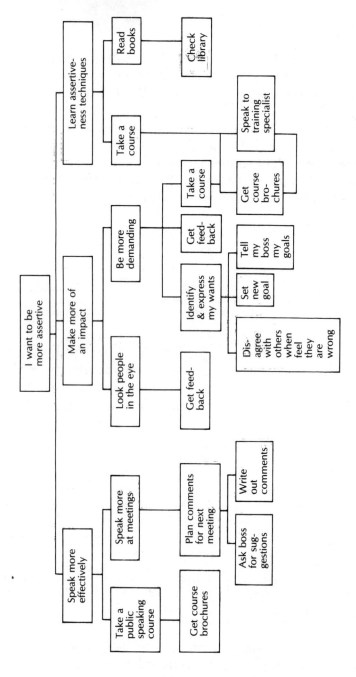

example, "How can I become more demanding?" One possibility would be to get feedback from teachers, managers, or
friends. Another might be to take an assertiveness training
course. (Note that if an alternative appears several times, it
suggests that it is worth pursuing because it is a means to
achieving several intermediate ends.) In any case, getting
feedback from your boss or taking a course are "doable"
things. The sample Means-Ends Analysis will now be completed. Very specific, doable steps which should be considered
now appear at the lower level of the chart.

Now, construct a Means-Ends Analysis on one of your
own goals.

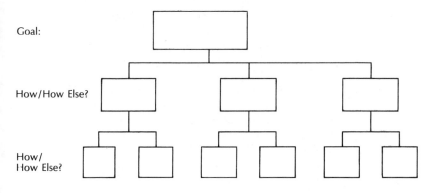

Add more boxes as needed. Keep going until you identify
"doable" things.

NEXT STEPS

In the next several chapters procedures, techniques and models for being more assertive and responsive will be identified.
These techniques provide the means by which you can achieve
your goals.

CHAPTER **5**

INTERACTION

INTERACTION: THE CORE OF EFFECTIVENESS

It is rare to achieve results without interaction. In the majority of important, interpersonal situations there is always a two-way flow of influence. It is unlikely that you can improve your ability to get things done without improving both your capacity to influence other people and your capacity to be responsive to others. With some exceptions, success in both business and social situations is dependent upon your capacity to be both a talker and a listener, one who initiates and presents points of view and who also explores and seeks out the points of view of others.

THE ASSERTIVE-RESPONSIVE HIERARCHY (A-R)

Therefore, it is useful to develop both assertive and responsive skills simultaneously, to integrate your capacities to influence others and to be influenced by them. The likelihood that you will achieve results, solve problems, and get what you want while at the same time maintaining sound relationships and support from others is increased by shaping your approach to the influence hierarchy. This hierarchy has four levels. Each level includes the possibility of behaving either assertively or responsively, or of combining assertive and responsive behavior.

The Assertive-Responsive Hierarchy

1. Exchange information (ideas and feelings)
2. Build understanding
3. Develop acceptance
4. Get action

This hierarchy is a model which defines key incremental steps which produce effective interaction. However, like all models, it cannot be applied rigidly. There are exceptions to the procedure and times when the sequence should be modified to fit the needs of a given situation. Nevertheless, in general, the step-by-step hierarchy is intended to apply to most interpersonal situations of importance.

The model suggests the following: First, the best way to begin to work through a problem is by exchanging information, presenting ideas and seeking out the ideas of others. By contrast, it is usually not advisable to take a fixed position or to express a specific goal or want before an exchange has occurred. For example, approaching your supervisor in a business situation and saying, "I want a 20 percent increase because I've been doing an outstanding job," expresses your goal without any exchange of information, without any exploration. The supervisor may not be prepared to discuss the issue at this time; the criteria for an increase may be unclear; perceptions of your performance may differ. A much more appropriate beginning would be something like, "I want to talk over my performance and my compensation."

Thus, it is desirable to move up the hierarchy one step at a time rather than jumping in by making your demands.

Information must be exchanged to build understanding. Understanding must be built to develop acceptance. This can lead to positive action. In the material which follows, each level of the assertiveness responsiveness hierarchy will be discussed in some detail.

LEVEL 1—EXCHANGE INFORMATION

As indicated, the best way to begin any significant interpersonal process is to exchange information. Whether you are going to ask for a raise, criticize a subordinate or associate, or refuse a demand placed on you, it is important to avoid taking a fixed position or beginning to "sell" benefits before clarification of the issues involved has occurred.

Assertiveness

Early in the discussion of significant issues, it is essential to keep channels open while presenting your point of view clearly, without apologies or self-deprecation. Here are some basic guidelines for being assertive in the early stages of a conversation.

1. Make your statements affirmative and brief—avoid hostile or apologetic behavior.
2. Avoid prematurely requesting action or moving towards a solution.
3. Deal with issues rather than personal needs or impressions.
4. Be descriptive rather than evaluative or judgmental.

It's important to note that these ingredients are particularly appropriate *early* in an exchange. Clearly, as you move through a discussion with another person, it may be necessary and desirable for you to point out your own personal opinions, to express your judgments and to make requests for positive action. Early in an encounter, however, it is much more appropriate to stay with descriptions of issues rather than personal statements of preference or needs. Here are some examples of desirable or OK assertions at this first level and undesirable or not OK assertions.

Appropriate Assertions	Inappropriate Assertions
"This article (watch, appliance, etc.) is not operating."	"If you don't give me my money back for this article, I'll sue your company."
"Class, I'm going to go over an important assignment with you. I want to be sure that it's clear and that you have an opportunity to ask questions. So let's review it."	"Class, here is an assignment that must be turned in on time. Anyone who doesn't turn it in will be simply proving that he/she isn't interested in this course."
"I have an idea that I think will benefit both of us. I'd like to discuss it with you."	"I have an idea. I know that you've got a lot more experience than I have, and I certainly don't want to be presumptuous, but I'd sure appreciate it if you'd give me a chance to go over this with you. I'm sure it needs a lot of improvement."
"You've been late several times this week" (supervisor to subordinate).	"Obviously you're not a very responsible person. You never come in on time."

These illustrations point out the appropriateness of being brief, affirmative and descriptive rather than prematurely demanding or critical of yourself or of others. Notice, too, that by being descriptive you avoid two serious pitfalls: (1) you don't place blame on the other person, thereby avoiding a defensive or hostile reaction from him/her; and (2) you don't place blame on yourself, thereby avoiding a wishy-washy, non-assertive or self-deprecatory stance.

There is usually a wide range of responses available to you in working on any kind of problem, no matter how complex or emotionally charged. If you remain positive and descriptive, you can avoid putdowns. A statement such as, "You haven't been handling this very well and I'm going to straighten it out. Here's my idea," is almost assured to put people off. Instead, a statement such as, "Here's an idea that I've experimented with that produced some very interesting results. I'd like to review it with you," invites an exchange of information and avoids putting the other person on the defensive. Even in an emotionally-charged situation you can avoid creating tension and hostility as long as you don't place blame. Here's an example of a negative approach to an emotional situation: "You're always putting me down and making me feel inadequate. I don't know why you don't treat me like you do other people in this group." A more positive approach would be: "I sometimes feel uncomfortable during group meetings. I'd like to talk over how we've been working together in group situations."

Responsiveness

Just as it is undesirable to take a strong position prematurely or push for results before you've exchanged information, it is equally undesirable to change your position or to "go along" with someone else before you have found out more about the issues at hand. Therefore, early in a problem-solving situation or when you are attempting to achieve a specific goal, it is highly desirable to seek information before modifying your position or showing acceptance of the other person's point of view. Here are considerations involved in being responsive at level 1—exchanging information.

1. Ask questions
2. Show concern for the other person's point of view
3. Keep the situation open (avoid early fixed positions)

One is often able to create a climate in which a problem can be solved and in which objections can be overcome by seeking information, by being responsive and showing a willingness to exchange ideas rather than by taking a fixed position. Following you will find a brief dialogue in which both parties stay at the first level of the Assertive-Responsive Hierarchy, thus keeping the situation open even though it is highly charged. The discussion involves a doctor and a nurse reviewing a breach of procedure during an operation.

DOCTOR: *As you know, this operation took about 20 minutes longer than usual.*

HEAD O.R. NURSE: *Yes, it was long. Were there any problems or difficulties that I should know about?*

DOCTOR: *Yes. During the operation a key procedure was omitted and we had to go back and repeat it and make corrections in the procedure.*

HEAD O.R. NURSE: *Yes, I noticed that change. It did seem unusual to me. What happened?*

DOCTOR: *Nurse X omitted a key step. I'd like to discuss what steps we can take to insure that the procedure is handled systematically, and review possible causes for the omission of the step.*

HEAD O.R. NURSE: *OK. When should we get together?*

In contrast, note a discussion in which individuals make premature judgments, place blame and do not keep the communication channels open.

DOCTOR: *One of your nurses made a bad mistake and it cost us 20 minutes in time. What's the matter with your people?*

HEAD O.R. NURSE: *My nurses are instructed to follow the doctor's request. A request was made for the third step in the procedure and that's what she did. If you want our nurses to take responsibility for the operation, then you'd better put them in charge of the procedure rather than making them lackeys for a bunch of egotistical residents.*

If the persons involved keep the situation open they may discover the cause of the issue and in many instances they can work through a mutually acceptable solution. Placing blame, putting other people down or simply apologizing for poor performance rarely contributes to improvements. Clearly, at some point the parties involved need to accept responsibility for developing a more appropriate course of action, but there is no reason for a win-lose battle around an issue which can only be resolved by mutual confidence and effort. It's important to recognize that these illustrations are somewhat unreal because the interaction between the two individuals has been portrayed as limited at the first level, that is, exchanging information. In complex situations it is appropriate to begin to build understanding and move towards acceptance. Some additional and more sophisticated techniques are involved.

LEVEL 2—BUILD UNDERSTANDING

The second level of the Assertive-Responsive Hierarchy involves building understanding. Once again, each individual must be both assertive and responsive if a genuine understanding of the issues is to occur. The key skill in asserting yourself with understanding is to use a response which builds in empathetic components. Empathy involves being aware of and tuned in to the feelings, needs, and points of view of others.

However, empathy is of little value unless it is demonstrated in behavior. Understanding assertions are often expressions of alternatives or options, thus implicitly recognizing the opportunity of the other to contribute and the potential for a two-way flow of influence between and among the parties. At this second level of communication it is again desirable to avoid fixed or dogmatic positions or a premature attempt to sell the benefits of your point of view.

Interactions

The second level provides the foundation for development of understanding and commitment. There is not a clear line of demarcation between exchanging information and building understanding. Rather, understanding flows from the exchange. Here are the key ingredients in the process of building understanding.

1. Clarify objectives
2. Develop alternatives
3. Use "active" listening

Clarify Objectives

One of the major obstacles to understanding occurs when the parties involved are not clear as to "where they're going." A great deal of tension and hostility occurs when people argue about issues which, even if they were settled, would not contribute to the solution of the problem at hand. Therefore, the most useful first step in building understanding—after some information has been exchanged—is to be clear about the purpose of the discussion at hand. That clarification of purpose or definition of objectives can be defined as identifying the conditions which the parties feel should exist in the future. By being clear as to where the discussion is going there is a much better chance of both parties contributing useful information and much less chance that people will waste energy on the wrong issues. One of the best ways of clarifying the process is to encourage the other party to identify the conditions he/she would like to have exist after the situation has been resolved.

For example, assume you are returning some merchandise with which you're dissatisfied. After describing the issue and exchanging information with the salesclerk or complaint department, it may then be appropriate to specify the conditions you wish to have exist when the situation is ended: "Well, I've described the problem and I think we both understand what happened. I'd like to have this merchandise replaced or get it fixed so that it will work properly." Or, "I think you understand the problem. This thing just isn't working properly. I'd like a refund." In each of these cases you have stated your objective. Obviously, in many situations the other person also has an objective which may be different from yours. The conversation might continue by your seeking to understand the other person's objectives. For example, "I think you understand that I want my money back. I'd like to understand your store's policy regarding damaged merchandise. How have these things been handled in the past?"

In some negotiating situations it is better not to probe too deeply into the reasons why a given course of action cannot be followed. Often it is more appropriate simply to be clear about your own objectives and push forward. However, in dealing with many problem-solving situations, and particularly in situations where joint commitment is important, it is appropriate to interact, to gather information about how the other person sees the purposes of the discussion as well as expressing your own point of view.

Develop Alternatives

One of the most significant obstacles to understanding and the development of a specific course of action is the presence of rigid positions on the part of one or both of the individuals involved. One way to avoid a rigid stance and also communicate a genuine problem-solving attitude is to offer and seek alternatives rather than merely stating a specific position.

Assume your goal in returning damaged merchandise is simply to solve the problem. You might suggest several alternatives such as, "Based on our discussion I'd like to do one of several things: either get my money back, get this equipment fixed, or get a replacement which you feel certain will work properly." You might probe for alternatives from the other individual, possibly by saying, "Do you see any other possibilities whereby this matter could be settled equitably?"

The return of merchandise is often a relatively trivial problem. The same process applies, however, in much more profound situations. For example, in the Cuban missile crisis described earlier (how would the U.S. respond to the movement of missiles into Cuba?) there was a great deal of consideration given to the development of objectives (what conditions do we want to exist after we act?) and then there was an exploration of alternatives to determine the possibilities which would lead to the desirable outcome. Clearly, the United States did not want a war with Russia. On the other hand, it did not want rockets based in Cuba only ninety miles off the coast of the U.S. Therefore, numerous alternatives were identified and explored in terms of the desired objectives or outcome. Throughout the interaction between the U.S. and Russian governments there was an attempt to keep communications open and to maintain a problem-solving orientation, even though the objectives of the two parties differed dramatically.

In the Cuban situation, and dozens of others, it becomes

clear that understanding is most apt to occur when partici-
pants in the discussion are genuinely willing to offer alternatives and at the same time consider alternatives offered by
others. Those in the discussion who take fixed positions rarely
contribute to a resolution of the issues at hand. However,
the problem-solving process should not be confused with the
need and desire on the part of many persons to maintain
their own convictions and to take a firm stand. There is almost
always more than one way to achieve what one wants and
you are much more likely to achieve understanding with others by keeping those options open. Further, by asking questions, probing and exploring the views of others you may be
able to extract additional alternatives even though the other
individuals seem to be taking a fixed position. Here is a brief
dialogue showing how you can generate alternatives by behaving assertively and responsively even with someone who is
highly resistant to change.

MANAGER: *The only way we're going to make any progress is
by reducing the cost of selling each unit. That can
be done by increasing our unit sales and by fewer
sales representatives making more calls.*

SUPERVISOR: *(Reporting to manager) I'd like to explore some of
the ways in which we might get sales representatives
to make more calls and also see if there are any
other ways in which we can increase our sales effectiveness. One thing that occurred to me was to provide sales representatives with some additional training and to set more specific goals regarding sales
calls.*

MANAGER: *I agree with you that we need to set higher goals
for our sales representatives. I'm not so sure about
the training program because it's going to cost us
more money and that means less profit.*

SUPERVISOR: *Well, if we could somehow find a way to get more
calls per sales representative without spending more*

> *money, that would certainly move in the direction we agree is desirable. One way of doing this would be to cut down the size of territories so that sales representatives would have less distance to travel and then set specific call goals for each representative.*

MANAGER: *But we'd need more sales representatives if we have more territories. However, that may be a way of increasing our volume. Why don't you prepare some recommendations for realignment of territories and allocating costs?*

By exploring alternatives the supervisor has participated with the manager in a way which may lead the manager to change his/her mind. Thus, the manager started out by saying that there was only one solution, yet ends up considering the possibility of adding more people, an alternative which seems diametrically opposed to his/her initial position. The supervisor presented and explored additional alternatives, avoided a fixed position, and avoided a win-lose attitude, thereby keeping the situation open and allowing new alternatives to surface.

In summary, then, an assertive-responsive approach to clarifying alternatives is a major element in developing understanding and building towards a positive course of action.

Use Active Listening

Finally, as indicated earlier in discussions of responsiveness, improvement in the quality of communications requires individuals to actively seek out and respond to the feelings, opinions, and ideas of others. This aspect of communication is particularly important during the process of building understanding and, specifically, in seeking out and offering alternatives. If your goal is to keep the situation open, then active listening is a major tool. Listening involves more than simply being silent, although that is often an appropriate way to encourage the other person to talk. It also involves asking questions and showing the other person that you understand his/her point of view by summarizing or reflecting back to that person. A third listening technique is to interpret what has been said as a way of clarifying it or moving it toward a higher level of understanding.

Here is an example of how active listening can be used to clarify alternatives.

STUDENT: *I've decided to drop Spanish. I just don't have any interest in foreign languages and I'm not doing well in it anyway.*

TEACHER: *I should like to get a better understanding of what's been happening to you in Spanish.*

STUDENT: *I find the language boring. I guess maybe I don't have any natural talent for languages.*

TEACHER: *Do you remember when you first began to feel it was boring?*

STUDENT: *Right at the start I didn't like it, and I was pretty tied up at the beginning of the term so I didn't have much chance to do homework and I fell behind.*

TEACHER: *So the whole thing started off in an unsatisfactory way.*

STUDENT: *That's right, and it's really embarrassing in class because I'm so far behind and I'm not able to answer questions or participate in the discussion.*

TEACHER: *I see. Well it sounds as though it's kind of a vicious circle. You got a little behind, you got tied up with other things, and now it seems impossible to catch up or at least in the process of catching up the situation may continue to be embarrassing.*

STUDENT: *Yes, I really hate dropping the course so late in the term because I'm going to need those credits later on. I suppose if there were some way to get some assistance and not be embarrassed in class, I might want to continue. But it just seems impossible at this point.*

The teacher has used a variety of active listening responses: asking questions, mirroring back, interpreting what has been said. At no time did the teacher express an opinion, make a judgment, or make a demand. The result is that the student is now exploring the issue in more depth and with a broader perspective. He/she may still decide to drop the course but there is a possibility now that he/she might consider getting special help, remedial assignments or some other means of catching up. Certainly the teacher's knowledge that embarrassment may be a key problem has increased the possibilities for a positive resolution of this dilemma.

By contrast, consider what can happen if a teacher does not keep the situation open, gives advice and fails to seek out the student's opinions.

STUDENT: *I've decided to drop Spanish. I just don't have any interest in foreign languages and I'm not doing well in it anyway.*

TEACHER: *I think you're making a serious mistake. You'll be losing time and credit and I'm perfectly willing to give you extra help if you need it.*

STUDENT: *I've thought it through and I've made up my mind. I just don't enjoy languages. I don't have much talent in that area.*

TEACHER: *The whole idea of having "language talent" is a myth. Anyone who really wants to can learn a language. What's happened is that you've let your work slide, you've gotten behind, and all you need to do is apply yourself and you can pass the course.*

STUDENT: *I know a lot of people who have a flair for language. They don't have to study very hard and they just seem to catch on right away. I think I can use my time more valuably by taking something which I enjoy and for which I have some ability.*

TEACHER: *Well, you're going to learn later in life that you can't just go after things that feel comfortable or that come*

> *easily to you. Every time you quit something it just*
> *diminishes your character.*
>
> STUDENT: *You make it sound as though dropping Spanish is going*
> *to mar me for life . . .*

In this instance the opportunity for resolution is diminished. The parties have gone down two different pathways, neither of which was particularly relevant to settling the issue.

Understanding is built when those involved expend their energies seeking out information from others, when they are able to listen and respond genuinely to opinions or points of view that are different from their own. In that process there are times when it is appropriate for one or both parties to express their own views clearly and affirmatively. Building understanding, however, is a gradual, cumulative process. It's important to recognize that although it takes two to build understanding, if one of the parties is skillful in drawing out the other, in listening and in responding affirmatively and assertively, then he/she can change a negative situation into a positive one.

Thus, in the initial illustration involving the teacher and the student, the teacher was applying effective listening methods. Although the student began with a somewhat negative and defensive posture, gradually his/her attitude changed as he/she asserted views without prejudice or defensiveness.

LEVEL 3—DEVELOP ACCEPTANCE

The next stage in effective interaction is to move from understanding towards acceptance or commitment. For example, in the earlier illustration it is possible that genuine understanding may develop between the teacher and the student. However, this does not assure that constructive action will occur. After the initial phases of exchanging information and an active listening process, alternatives may emerge. These might include: the student may drop the course, the student may seek and receive special help, the student might continue the course without credit to reduce pressure and subsequently sign up for it again later. Special assignments, special classes, a redefinition of the student's role in the classroom are all possibilities.

Understanding of these possibilities is not enough. A course of action must be specified and worked through. The steps in gaining acceptance are:

1. Weigh alternatives
2. Clarify the consequences of any given choice
3. Apply the assertiveness planning model:
   a. Set a specific, measurable, "doable," timed goal
   b. Decide on a pathway to the goal
   c. Know the techniques for achieving the goal
   d. Identify and apply your own resources

Weight Alternatives

As mentioned earlier, it is desirable to avoid value judgments and fixed positions in the early stages of a problem-solving or decision-making discussion or in counseling or interviewing others. However, after an initial exchange of information and the development of understanding, it is then necessary to begin to develop acceptance for a specific course of action. This means that alternatives which were surfaced in earlier portions of the discussion must now be pinned down. They must be evaluated and decisions about them must be made.

In part, this can be done simply by exchanging points of view or attitudes regarding various alternatives. In some instances this is a rather simple process wherein each individual states the pros and cons of a given course of action as he/she sees them. The reasons for choosing a particular course of action may pop out fairly readily. In other instances, a more careful and systematic analysis of the alternatives may be necessary.

Suppose a piece of equipment breaks down—an office machine, a household appliance, a car—and you have to decide with another person what to do. Three alternatives might appear to be available:

1. We can repair and maintain the present equipment.
2. We can lease a piece of equipment similar to the one we now have but in better shape.
3. We can buy a new piece of equipment.

A quick examination of these options may reveal that both parties agree that it is more economical and rewarding to buy the new equipment. However, if the decision is not readily apparent and if the potential cost is significant, it may be desirable to make a more thorough analysis.

One way to facilitate decisions is to use a "decision chart." A chart is constructed by listing the alternatives down the left-hand side in the boxes, shown on the next page, and then identifying the major criteria across the top. The criteria are the basis for weighing the alternatives and making the decision. Usually these include considerations of cost, satisfaction (not only personal satisfaction but the degree to which the decision solves the problem and meets the need), and feasibility (how readily can we do it?). The chart can be completed by putting in numbers for the costs and satisfaction, for example, savings or profits, or by assigning "high," "medium" or "low" ratings to the boxes when it is not easy to insert figures. For purposes of illustration, suppose that leasing new equipment would cost more than rebuilding the old equipment or purchasing new equipment. Satisfaction with leased equipment may not be as high as with purchased equipment, however, though certainly more than with repaired equipment which can be expected to break down in the future. The feasibility of maintaining and servicing the old equipment may be low; that is, necessary spare parts, skilled service people and reliable maintenance arrangements may not be feasible. Given these factors, the decision chart looks like this:

| | Criteria | | |
Alternatives	Cost	Satisfaction	Feasibility
Repair & maintain old equipment	low	low	low
Lease new equipment	high	moderate	high
Buy new equipment	moderate	high	high

What is wanted? Very simply, we want to choose an alternative which is low in cost, high in satisfaction, and high in feasbility. The repair alternative can be eliminated immediately because it produces little satisfaction and is not particularly feasible, anyway. The lease is the highest cost option and is coupled with moderate satisfaction, making that choice rather doubtful. The buy choice seems to have the best chance of working out for you since it provides a high degree of satisfaction at a moderate cost and it is highly feasible.

Examine Consequences

In many instances, interacting with others in a genuine assertive and responsive fashion means that you must dig into the issues more deeply. This can be done by going beyond the "decision chart" and more carefully examining the consequences of a given course of action. Consider, again, the student who is thinking about quitting the Spanish course. After an initial exchange of information and a gradual development of understanding, it may be useful for the teacher to begin to examine with the student the consequences of the various alternatives that have been discussed. The discussion might go something like this:

TEACHER: *If you stay in the course, I'll be willing to spend extra time with you and we'll arrange assignments so that you'll not find the situation embarrassing. The result is that you will benefit from the time you've already spent in the course, you'll get the credits I think you feel are desirable, and I'm hopeful you'll even find that Spanish can be reasonably enjoyable once you get into it.*

STUDENT: *Yes, I am concerned about wasting time and I do want to get credits as best I can.*

TEACHER: *I think you should examine what happens if you aren't able to connect with a language. Part of the problem you experienced in Spanish can occur in the study of any language; that is, if you get the rudiments piece by piece you suddenly find that you're way behind.*

STUDENT: *I suppose that's true. I really wish I could avoid languages, but I know they're necessary.*

TEACHER: *The college you've chosen does require a language, so one of the results of dropping out now is that you'll have to double up somewhere along the line in order to pick up the credits you'll need. That could be a big burden in your senior year when you'll want to get into a lot of activities that are enjoyable and part of being a senior.*

In this exchange, then, the parties begin to zero in on a specific solution. This is done by reviewing the consequences of the alternatives. The teacher points out the positive benefits of one course of action and the negative consequences associated with an alternative that is less desirable.

Acceptance can be developed by pointing out the advantages or disadvantages of a given course of action. In some instances acceptance may emerge more readily by encouraging the other individual to explore the consequences of his/

her choices rather than by "selling" a given position which you favor. In any case, one of the skills involved in being assertive is the capacity to present the benefits and, in some instances, the negative consequences of a given course of action in a way which does not evoke defensiveness or hostility.

Here's an instance when an employee (student, associate, professional) has been doing work of a quality which is not acceptable. Assume that the issue has been explored, information has been exchanged, understanding has been developed and the time has come to zero in on an acceptable course of action. The discussion might go something like this:

MANAGER: *We've discussed the fact that you haven't been satisfied with your job and that it has resulted in some results that neither of us are quite satisfied with.*

SUBORDINATE: *Continues Yes, that's true. I feel that if the work situation was more challenging and interesting, then I'd be able to get more involved and produce better results.*

MANAGER: *Right, and we agreed that there were several alternatives. One possibility is reassignment or job rotation. Another possibility is some retraining for a new kind of work. However, we agreed that in the short run it is essential to establish a good performance in your current job and we talked about some of the ways of doing that. Let's push a little further. What steps do you see that either or both of us can take to get moving on this?*

SUBORDINATE: *I'd like to begin some retraining activities, learning some new things, even as I tighten up my performance on the present job.*

MANAGER: *That sounds good to me. It is extremely important that we are mutually clear about performance in your present assignment being brought up to the level we both agree is desirable and maintained even as you gradually get involved in other activities.*

Notice that as the discussion occurs both parties are being assertive. Both are involved in continuing the process of clarifying issues while gradually moving toward more specific courses of action. Here are two brief comparative ways in which the situation might have been handled, one leading toward conflict and hostility and the other leading toward a rather loosely defined situation without clear direction.

Example 1—Conflict

SUBORDINATE: (Continues) *Yes, I'd particularly like to get some new assignments or a chance for retraining.*

MANAGER: *Well, look, you shouldn't be asking for these new and special things until you've proven to me that you can do your present job adequately.*

SUBORDINATE: *I thought our purpose today was to solve this problem, not to treat me like I had been irresponsible. I gave you the reasons why things hadn't been going well. I think you and the organization are just as much to blame as I am.*

Note that in the earlier example the manager was able to make an affirmative, assertive statement about job requirements without alienating the subordinate and without making undue commitments or promises for new assignments or new work.

Example 2—Lack of Direction

SUBORDINATE: *Yes, and I'd particularly like to get some new assignments or a chance for retraining.*

MANAGER: *Well, what would you like to do?*

SUBORDINATE: *I'd like to get into job X. I know it requires more skill and there's a chance to make more money.*

MANAGER: *OK, you start working on that and we'll talk about it again pretty soon.*

In this instance the manager did not make it clear that performance on the present job was the first criterion for success nor did he/she specify the steps to be taken in order to develop in the new area. The employee might well leave the situation feeling that he/she was not expected to make significant improvements in the present job and without any clear idea as to how to proceed into a new job or improve his/her skills. It is essential that both parties be clear about what will happen. The planning process facilitates clarity.

Apply the Planning Model

The last step in the process of developing acceptance is to apply the model that was referred to in some detail in Chapter 4. The model began to appear in the positive illustration used on page 87; that is, those involved were setting goals, they were beginning to talk through ways of getting to those goals.

GET ACTION

The final step in the assertive-responsive interactive process moves the parties to obtain positive action. In many ways action occurs as a result of the previous three steps. That is, individuals involved have exchanged appropriate information. If they understand the issues and if they have accepted the need to act, action can emerge naturally. However, in many such instances action does not take place. The way to insure that positive action occurs is to give consideration to the following elements:

1. Be sure the action steps are "doable."
2. Be sure there's agreement not only on what should be done but on how it will be done, when it will be done, and how it will be measured.

3. Provide for feedback and follow-up so that results can be measured and assessed.

Specify Doable Action Steps

As emphasized in Chapter 4, constructive action is more likely to occur when programs, goals, and courses of action are reduced to "doable" steps. The fact that you may reach an agreement with someone does not mean that he/she will act on that agreement. For example, assume you and another person agree that you will get together more frequently to discuss matters of mutual concern. This won't happen unless you convert it into "doable" steps. That is, there has to be a time, a place, a specific agenda to increase the likelihood that these discussions will occur. Consider how often you have said to someone, "Yes, we should get together for dinner sometime." Obviously, that will not occur unless it is made "doable" and specific. The same is true of more profound issues.

The process, then, of developing a pathway—particularly for a long-term or complex goal—requires that the individual involved make specific choices that will move him/her toward the goal. In order to achieve results with others, it is essential to be assertive and responsive as you begin to move closer to working out specific action plans. For example, you will rarely get what you want in a given situation involving others unless you assertively and responsively clarify the pathways toward the goal and develop commitment (or choices) from yourself and others regarding what will be done. Here's an example of an individual discussing his/her job future with an immediate superior.

SUBORDINATE: *I just wanted to let you know that I feel I've been doing quite a good job and I would like to get ahead.*

MANAGER: *Well, you are doing quite well and don't worry. In this company people are always rewarded for good performance.*

SUBORDINATE: *I appreciate that. I just wanted to be sure that you know that I am concerned about the future and that I want to do whatever I can to make progress.*

MANAGER: *Well, that's good, and I admire your concern. Keep at it. Your future looks quite good.*

The chances are that if the conversation ends here the subordinate is left with a feeling of some doubt as to his/her future. The subordinate may be aware of the fact that he/she has not been particularly assertive, nor were responsive techniques used in order to specify a course of action. If the subordinate asserts him/herself in developing goals and seeks out or is responsive to the manager in attempting to clarify alternatives, then the conversation moves along quite differently. Secondly, if the subordinate engages the manager in the development of pathways toward his/her goals, then a more significant interaction occurs. Both parties become increasingly assertive, clear and straightforward about the possibilities that are present. Here's how such a discussion might sound.

SUBORDINATE: *I'd like to talk over my performance with you today. I feel I've been getting good results. I'd like to know how you see them and get suggestions for improvement.*

MANAGER: *Well, I'm pleased that you're concerned about this. Don't worry. You're doing a good job and this company will certainly respond to you when good results are produced.*

SUBORDINATE: *I appreciate that and I'd like to pursue it a little further. What specific steps do you feel I need to take in order to improve my current performance?*

MANAGER: *As I said, you're doing quite well. It just takes time.*

SUBORDINATE: *It would be extremely helpful for me to know what you see to be a high level of performance so that I can work toward that level more directly.*

MANAGER: *We consider someone to be performing well when, among other things, he/she is able to answer technical problems quickly and accurately.*

SUBORDINATE: *I see. Technical knowledge is clearly important in performing well. Do you feel it's a part of what I need in order to move ahead in responsibility and to be considered for promotions in the future?*

MANAGER: *Well, certainly, that's a factor that's considered when a promotional opening is present. It's also important to demonstrate the capacity to get results through other people.*

SUBORDINATE: *How do you feel I've been doing in that area?*

MANAGER: *Well, you've been getting some cooperation, but I'd like to see you get more vigorous support and involvement from the people working with you.*

SUBORDINATE: *As you know, last week Phil Smith and I disagreed as to how job X should be carried out. I felt it was important to pursue that problem despite the disagreement. I would be interested to know whether you felt my performance in pushing for results with other people was effective.*

MANAGER: *I think you put your finger on an area of concern to me. You are sometimes abrasive in dealing with other people. I don't want to talk about Phil but, in general, if you rub people the wrong way, you're not going to have them with you over the long run.*

SUBORDINATE: *Then one of my goals might be to work with people so they are more cooperative. I'd like to talk more about that. I want to push for results and I want to keep people with me. That seems to me to be a goal to push for in the next couple of months.*

MANAGER: *Yes, I agree. I want to emphasize that the genuine*

> *measure of your performance is the results you achieve, but those results have to be looked at in a long-term way. I feel you'll be performing well in this area when the people you work with feel they "own" part of the projects they're involved in, when they are enthusiastic about what they're doing. Right now they seem willing to take directions from you but they don't really seem involved.*

Although the subordinate is perhaps hearing some things he/she would rather not hear, that is, he/she is somewhat abrasive, is not getting as much involvement as possible, etc., there is little chance that the subordinate will get ahead until these issues are handled effectively. By being assertive and responsive with the boss, the subordinate has begun to establish a basis for moving toward his/her goals. You will notice, too, that the boss becomes more assertive, he/she is beginning to make both suggestions and develop some commitment, for example, "I feel you'll be performing well in this area when. . ." Thus, the conditions that are desirable in the future are being spelled out; objectives are being established.

When an open exchange of information occurs, when one or both of the persons involved shows understanding and seeks out the views of the other, when the parties develop alternatives, explore and decide those alternatives and gradually move toward specific courses of action, then the chances of achieving results are greatly enhanced.

Determine How and How Well

Although identifying and breaking tasks down into "doable" components is critical to effective action, the components also have to be converted into measurable units. The best way to deal with this issue is to ask a question, "How will we know when this task has been accomplished successfully?" For example, suppose in a medical installation that it is agreed that the relationship between medical staff and paramedical or service staff needs to be improved and that weekly meetings will be held and several joint task forces will be formed towards that end. These steps do not insure that the desired results will occur. Some measurement of performance is needed in answer to the question, "How will we know when the relationship between medical and nonmedical staff has improved?" In a sense this second step involves developing agreed-upon criteria or measurements of success. Someone might say, "Well, one thing for sure is that if we get fewer formal complaints from the nonmedical staff, we'll know things are better." Someone else might say, "When the medical staff finds the materials, reports, and support service they need are available when they need them, that will be an indication that there's more cooperation."

Note that these indicators of success can be converted into specific goals which further enhance the opportunities to achieve results. Unfortunately, many individuals assume that by being assertive they are going to produce results. The fact is that assertiveness needs to be coupled with appropriate methodology and content. Therefore, saying to someone, "I want you to be on time," is an assertion but unless that assertion is made "doable," unless both parties agree as to what is reasonable, what the criteria are, then the chances are that success will not occur.

Provide for Feedback and Follow-Up

For the most part new methods work best when there are built-in, self-correcting features. For example, assume you feel you want to lose weight. You've translated your goal into something "doable;" that is, "I'm going to eat 10 percent less calories per day." You know what you're going to do and you then determine how it will be done and how it will be measured, for example, cut out bread and potatoes and eat no desserts. The final step in determining whether the system is working is feedback itself. This is provided by getting on a scale periodically and finding out whether actual weight loss is occurring. If it's not occurring, it means that you're not living up to the goals you agreed upon or that you defined the problem wrongly. You may have to reemphasize the goals, get further help in carrying them out, develop new dieting methods, or establish another follow-up program to insure that you stay on the track you have designed for yourself.

This same procedure applies to being assertive with a subordinate who is not performing well, solving problems with friends or spouses, and working with others to achieve your or their objectives. It's not enough to identify what should be done. It's important to develop feedback mechanisms and to provide for continuing review and assessment in order to insure that the effort agreed upon stays on the track.

SUMMARY

Assertive-responsive behavior is more than simply a "style." It is more than a way of talking or a physical attitude. Although it usually involves looking people in the eye, standing up straight, talking with conviction, and listening in a responsive way, this may not be enough. The framework or model presented here includes the application of carefully-considered and well-established problem-solving methods. Even the most timid or shy individual can increase his/her assertive-responsive effectiveness by clarifying or contributing to the clarification of objectives and by seeking out alternatives from others. Individuals who may come across as abrasive or aggressive because of their tone of voice or general attitude can become more assertive and responsive by working with others to develop pathways toward goals rather than simply stating those goals. Thus, assertiveness and responsiveness are more than a style or set of superficial behaviors. They are a way of working with people, a way of drawing upon the resources of others and utilizing your own resources to determine what should be done and to work out action plans for doing it.

CHAPTER **6**

HOW TO

HOW VERSUS WHAT

The preceding chapter provided you with a basis for determining *what* should be done in order to achieve results. Thus, it's important to exchange information, develop understanding, build acceptance, and establish ways of taking action. To some degree, these elements were illustrated with some of the "how to's" of assertive-responsive behavior. However, there are increasingly specific modes of action available to you as you begin to zero in on what needs to be done. There is a relationship between means and ends. If you wish to clarify objectives, there are ways of making that process more effective. If you wish to listen more accurately, there are ways of listening that can be identified and practiced. This chapter describes the "how to's," the sets of skills that are needed in order to behave in an assertive and responsive style.

You will note that in almost every aspect of problem solving and decision making, indeed in most day-to-day activities which involve two or more individuals, it is essential to clarify objectives, to search out and develop understanding of goals, and in general to keep the situation open until a specific course of action can be worked out. *In every new or complicated situation it is essential to begin by clarifying what's going on.* The skills associated with this aspect of assertiveness can be defined in a model or checklist.

How to Clarify Problems and Events

1. Describe events as you see them
2. Explore the views of others
3. Generate alternatives
4. Use open communication methods

A second basic model or set of "how to" skills is concerned with making choices and producing action.

How to Produce Action

1. Be concrete
2. Be firm and straightforward
3. Be convincing
4. Maintain a grounded position
5. Express wants and goals
6. Set targets

These two sets of skills are described and illustrated in this chapter. The final and extremely important area of assertiveness having to do with dealing with conflict and resistance will be dealt with in the chapter that follows.

SKILL SET 1—HOW TO CLARIFY PROBLEMS AND EVENTS

Describe Events

Whenever you are involved in exchanging information and building the basis for problem solving and decision making, whenever you are concerned with moving toward the development of a specific goal or course of action, it is essential to begin by being clear about "what's happening" now. There is a strong temptation in almost every situation in which you have vested interest to push towards a predetermined goal, to make a judgment about what's going on, to ask for action prematurely. The trouble is that premature judgments about factors which affect others are apt to slow down the problem-solving process. In order to avoid these pitfalls and build affirmative action, you need to begin by being descriptive rather than evaluative. This is accomplished by first identifying what's going on in neutral and unbiased terms. Rather than talking about how this is done, here are some exercises to aid you in identifying and practicing this skill.

Situation 1

You are bothered by the fact that an area in which you work (home, business, store) is cluttered. Others who use this same space (family members, business associates, co-workers) have contributed to this clutter. In order to make the exercise specific, assume that you are a supervisor and one of the people who works with you can, in your opinion, contribute to making the environment more pleasant and orderly. Which of the statements below might you make to begin involving this person in solving the problem?

1. I don't know if you've noticed, but this place is a mess and I think you better do something to get it cleaned up.
2. I think it's desirable to have an orderly and well arranged work place. Would you be willing to work with me to get this place cleaned up?
3. I think the way this place is set up makes it almost impossible to get anything done. You aren't going to get good results until you get this place straightened out.
4. I notice that there are quite a few boxes stacked around various work places and that surplus materials are stacked up along the wall.

Rank those statements 1, 2, 3, 4 in order of your preference. Which do you think is the best way of dealing with the situation and which is the worst? How do the other two fit in?

Comparative Analysis

Most people agree that statements 2 and 4 are more positive than 1 and 3. In applying step 1 of the model, that is, being descriptive, statements 2 and 4 come closest to a nonevaluative, descriptive way of dealing with this problem. Notice that statement 1 uses the term "mess" and is a strong expression of one person's perception or bias as to how the place looks. In reality, others who work in the same environment may feel that it is simply a busy place with quite a few useful materials stacked or ready to use. From your own experience you may know that some of the people you work with are not bothered by cluttered desks or the sloppy stacking of materials. They may, in fact, feel they work more effectively under the circumstances. You may increase their defensiveness and resistance if you refer to the place as messy or disorderly or ask, "How can anybody get anything done here?" In addition, it's important to consider the possibility that you may be wrong. What appears to you as messy or cluttered may be a necessary way of working with certain kinds of materials or situations. It may be that it is the result of a commitment on the part of a work group to get things done even though there is inadequate space or facilities. Others involved might well respond by saying or thinking, "Here we are working with inadequate space and inadequate materials. We're getting the work out on time, everybody's conscientious, and now we're going to be criticized because we have boxes stacked up."

Note that the difference between statement 2 and statement 4 is that statement 2 makes assumptions about what should be done; that is, the speaker has already determined that the place needs to be changed. He/she is simply asking the other person to accept the assumption and work together to change it. On the other hand, statement 4 does not presume that changes should be made, does not presume that a goal should be set. Rather, it describes the situation and makes it possible for the other person to become involved in assessing what's going on. Clearly, even statement 4 may result in some defensiveness. The individual may be thinking, "Well, I guess I'm going to be criticized for not cleaning up the place properly." Nevertheless, the speaker has not made any presumptions and can deal with resistance by maintaining a descriptive and problem-solving mode.

Explore the Views of Others

Notice, too, that by describing the situation rather than evaluating it the speaker has not "set up" the other person to either resist or accept the position that has been expressed. In addition, the initiator of the conversation can explore the other person's viewpoint without prejudice. For example, if you say to an individual, "Your work place is messy," then there is very little left to explore and, in fact, very little for the other person to do except to accept your point of view or to become defensive or resistant.

In the illustration which follows, descriptive statements can be combined with an exploration or seeking out of the other person's point of view. Again, identify which of the following statements you think works best. In this instance assume a teacher is concerned about cluttered desks and work tables.

1. Most people in the room have cluttered desks. This makes it difficult to avoid wrinkling papers and to maintain a good working area. How do you feel about this?

2. I'm sick and tired of seeing this place cluttered up. I wish you'd tell me why you won't get your materials organized and clean the place up.
3. I notice that many people's desks are full. There seems to be limited work space. Do you feel you have too many materials to store? Perhaps the amount of material creates no problem for you. In any case, I'd like to discuss whether we are using our space to the best advantage.
4. I think each person's place can be kept the way he or she chooses. I don't want to nag you or suggest that I know what's best for you, but I would like to explore whether we should clean things up a little bit. Would you mind?

Once again, rank the statements.

Comparative Analysis

Statement 4 introduces a new element in the process of describing or relating to the problem situation. In this instance, the individual becomes nonassertive, apologetic and tentative. Note that this is not a description of what's going on or a request for information. Rather, it is almost a plea for people not to object and to accept that the speaker is a "nice person." So if you found yourself attracted to this response, you might think back to other similar situations and ask yourself whether you are facilitating problem solving and your own interests or whether you are being overly apologetic and nonassertive.

Of the other three statements, in statement 1 the speaker seems to be "setting up" the students. The speaker has already identified that the situation is "bad" and then asks for opinions; this hardly seems the way to begin an open problem-solving discussion. Statement 2 is an attack. It is aggressive and would tend to create resistance. Statement 3 is descriptive. It explores the situation; it encourages an open approach.

In summary, it is important to recognize that exploration is a sound and useful communication mechanism. It involves other people, it opens the situation up, it provides the opportunity for you to receive new information and to become clearer about the viewpoints of others. It avoids the pitfalls of prematurely enforcing your view on another who may then become resistant or belligerent. It avoids the possibility of coming to conclusions too quickly without having adequate information. It shows respect and concern for the other person's point of view. However, exploration does not work if it is used to "entrap" other individuals by asking them questions which are aimed at leading them toward the decision you favor.

In using descriptive and explorative approaches, the underlying conviction and assumption must be "I may not know the right answer. I may have a point of view as to what's right. I may have an impression or I may have experience which leads me toward a given conclusion, but I do not know for sure what is correct until I have gethered information and clarified the awareness, perceptions, and attitudes of others." This does not mean that I am simply to be influenced by whatever anyone else thinks. It means that I am open to explore the facts and opinions that are present before determining what should be done.

Generate Alternatives

As indicated in earlier chapters, one of the most crucial steps in any problem-solving or decision-making effort, in any communication between individuals, is to develop alternatives rather than permaturely deciding on a course of action which may be proven later to be inadequate or inappropriate.

In almost every situation you face you mentally go through the process of considering alternatives. What shirt or blouse should you wear this morning? What do you wish to have for breakfast? What can you do to get more support from your boss? How can you improve your relationships with co-workers or family members? As you explore each instance in your mind you find yourself identifying options or possibilities before making a choice. Whether one is simply deciding "should I have eggs or cereal for breakfast?" or "should I confront the boss with my dissatisfaction or should I go along with what he/she has requested?", you are involved in surfacing and considering alternatives.

By definition, assertive behavior is an expression of what you want. Often there is a temptation to avoid the consideration of alternatives since this may come across as weakness and lack of confidence. However, in any situation in which you want to clarify what's going on and gather data in preparation for making a decision, it is appropriate and assertive to push for an examination of alternatives. Your stance may be extremely strong such as, "I do not want to make a decision until we have identified and reviewed all of the options we can think of," or it can be relatively tentative, "I'd like to continue exploring some other possibilities before we decide what to do."

Use Open Communication Methods

An individual is seen as being open when he/she is clear without being abrupt or harsh and without being wishy-washy or apologetic. Notice the differences among the statements which follow:

> *"You must be on time in the future."*
>
> *"I should like you to be on time in the future."*
>
> *"Please try to be on time in the future."*
>
> *"It's extremely important for you to be on time."*
>
> *"I want you to be on time."*

These statements differ in content, in the relationship connoted between the speaker and the receiver, and probably in the message received. Further differences may be conveyed by the speaker's tone of voice, posture, and the look on his/her face.

It is certainly inappropriate for one to be constantly involved in analyzing every word spoken or every expression used in communicating with others. It is important, however, to make careful distinctions among straightforward modes of communication, tentative and apologetic modes of communications, and dogmatic or presumptuous modes of communication. During the clarification phase it is desirable to be firm and clear without falling into the trap of inappropriate apology or unnecessary harshness. It is generally better to avoid highly tentative statements such as, "I think you can if you try," or "I'd like you to try," or "Please do me a favor and see if you can." It is equally desirable to avoid the other extreme such as, "You can if you're willing to exert yourself," or "you would if you really cared about your job," or "You've been late six times in the last eight weeks and I will not permit you to be late again." More extreme are threats, negative sanctions, pressure, and strong fixed positions which, for the most part, are not appropriate during the clarification process.

An open communication describes what has happened or what you would like to have happen without setting up a firm goal or demand. It is appropriate to express what you want if you genuinely want something to be done. For example, "You've been late six times in the last eight weeks. I want you to be on time," is an appropriate statement if there is an understanding of job requirements.

A middle ground in some highly-charged situations is to depersonalize your comments to some extent and refer to situational requirements. You might say, for example, "It's important to achieve quality standards," or "The flow of work requires that the person on this job be on time," or "It's important to review your scholastic record to determine how it might affect your future." However, as quickly as possible one should move to the personal communication, the "I" form, without being overbearing or presumptuous. There is a great deal of difference between saying "It's important to achieve quality standards" and "I cannot accept substandard quality from you."

Here are some sample situations. You are asked to write a brief response to each situation considering the suggestions that have been discussed.

Situation 1

Someone you are associated with has been spending too much money on "miscellaneous items." For example, in a family situation perhaps too much money is being spent on entertainment or other factors in the budget aside from the basic requirements (rent, food, etc.). The other person, in your opinion, is not living up to budget requirements that you and he/she have discussed in the past. How would you begin a discussion of this conversation? Write a brief statement aimed at initiating a conversation regarding inappropriate expenditures. Choose your own situation, that is, you might be talking to a family member, discussing a child's allowance, or initiating a discussion with a business associate or subordinate. Write out your statement.

_____

_____

_____

_____

Following is a checklist to aid you in analyzing your statement. It's broken down into desirable and undesirable characteristics. Look over the statement and see how many of the desirable characteristics are present. Check for undesirable characteristics. Based on that analysis you may wish to rewrite the statement.

Desirable Characteristics

_____ Describes the situation without judging or evaluating it

_____ Is brief and straightforward

_____ Contains no personal evaluations (of the situation or the other person)

_____ Contains an opportunity for the other person to respond

_____ Avoids "negative" or loaded terms (careless, too much, over budget)

Undesirable Characteristics

_____ Presumes that the speaker knows what's right

_____ Presumes the other person is wrong or careless

_____ Leaves little room for disagreement or discussion

_____ Puts the other person down

_____ Presumes the other person is to blame

_____ Contains a predetermined solution or course of action

Based on both checklists, rewrite the statement to communicate your concern with the budget in a way that eliminates the undesirable features and incorporates other desired features.

_____

_____

_____

_____

_____

Comparative Analysis

For comparison, here are some alternatives which are built around the checklists.

Example 1: I noticed that we have been spending more on miscellaneous items in the last couple of months than we have in the past. Perhaps there have been some changes in our situation or requirements. In any case, I'd like to discuss the situation.

Example 2: I want to discuss the budget with you. I know there have been some changes in expenditures and I'd like to go over our plans for the future.

Example 3: The budget shows that you have spent more on miscellaneous items than originally budgeted. Tell me what changes have occurred.

Here are some undesirable statements.

Example 1: You've been spending more money on miscellaneous items than you used to. I think you should tighten up.

Example 2: You've been spending too much money on miscellaneous items. Let's talk about how we can reduce it.

You may feel that both of these statements are OK. However, in line with the checklist and with basic communication skills, consider the following explanations.

When you say something like, "You've been spending too much" or "We've been spending too much" you are overlooking the posibility that there may be legitimate causes that you do not understand or about which you do not have information. Expenditures for miscellaneous items may have been high this time only to take advantage of a special sale or quantity discounts, to obtain better service, or to respond to a unique opportunity or risk. The assumption that too much was spent is premature unless one knows the nature of the expenditure, the causes for it, and the factors which influenced the decision. Dozens of illustrations can be given in almost any field. A salesman who says "Model A is better for you than Model B" without first describing the benefits of his/her proposal and exploring your needs and concerns may make an inappropriate judgment and thereby lose a sale. An individual who assumes he/she has the right answer or right course of action may block exploration of other more desirable courses of action.

Here is another problem situation for your consideration.

Situation 2

Someone associated with you has been very critical and abrasive in several situations. You are now currently facing that person privately. Once again, he/she says something demeaning or hostile, a statement like, "Well, once again your department has loused up. You just don't seem to be able to do anything right." Or, "I'm sick and tired of the way you treat the children. You're much too lenient and you don't seem to care what happens to them."

Assume that statements like this have been made in the past and in the presence of other people. For purposes of this illustration one sample statement will be used. The person says to you, "All you care about is yourself. You're never really willing to cooperate or you just back off and fail to make decisions. I'm fed up."

Write a response to this situation considering the checklists shown earlier.

_____

_____

_____

_____

Comparative Analysis

Notice in reviewing your statement that there is a strong temptation to put the other person down, to say something like "Who do you think you are?", or "You can't talk to me that way," or "Stop being so presumptuous." There is, on the other hand, the danger of responding with inappropriate niceness or softness. When someone puts you down or embarrasses you, it is usually not desirable to respond apologetically with a statement such as, "I'm awfully sorry that my behavior has bothered you. I'll certainly try to behave differently in the future."

Clearly, if you are wrong and wish to be clear about that, such a statement can be made. It need not be made in a self-demeaning or highly apologetic fashion. You might say something like, "I'm concerned that I've come across to you as selfish and unconcerned." In the preceding case, however, the presumption is that you have not been to blame. Therefore, your response might sound something like any of those shown below and on the following page:

Example 1: "I contribute and take action in situations which I have knowledge about and which I feel should be acted upon. Evidently you see my behavior as withdrawn or indifferent. That is not the case and I'd like to explore what's been happening."

Example 2: "I disagree with the way in which you see the situation. However, we can certainly discuss that disagreement. I don't like to be criticized in the presence of others when, in my opinion, the criticism is unfounded."

Example 3: "Evidently some of the things I've been doing bother you. I feel strongly that I'm operating appropriately and effectively. I do want to understand your point of view, so tell me more about how you see things."

Example 4: "It makes me angry when you criticize me and put me down. I think your comments are off the mark. What is it that's bothering you?"

Notice that it is appropriate to express your feelings (based on your own judgment as to the risks involved) and that feelings can be expressed straightforwardly and without hostility or patronization. Saying to someone, "I feel angry" or "It bothers me when you criticize me in public" is neither aggressive nor nonassertive behavior. It is assertive and may be appropriate. You may wish to keep the situation somewhat neutral by simply giving information, for example, "I am carrying out the job based on the goals and objectives I established with others early in the game. If my actions cause problems for you, let's talk about it." This in no way demeans you nor demeans the other person. It expresses your point of view without a great deal of emotionality.

Keep in mind that all of these responses are desirable during the clarification phase of any discussion. Later on you may want to specify courses of action. You may want to say something like, "I do not want to be criticized in the presence of my staff again" or "Unless we can reach agreement on how to handle this situation, I suggest we sit down with the boss and work it through," or "There's a great deal to be gained by both of us finding ways to cooperate. I don't expect to back down nor do I expect you to back down. Rather, I want both of us to begin cooperating immediately on current tasks and problems."

All of the statements in the preceding paragraph can be appropriate. Note, however, that they tend to jump too quickly to solutions and specify action unless the situation has been clarified through a thorough exchange of information

and unless some acceptance and commitment has developed
on the need for action.

SKILL SET 2—HOW TO
PRODUCE ACTION

The second major skill set applies to the process whereby
you move towards action. This is done by being concrete,
firm, and convincing; by expressing your wants and goals
clearly in a "grounded" style; and by setting targets.

Be Concrete

Early in a conversation it may be desirable to generalize somewhat and to keep the situation open. For example, "I want
to discuss ways in which we can improve cost effectiveness"
is a typical opening, a general statement. After discussion,
after alternatives have been developed as you begin to move
toward making decisions and being specific, it is then appropriate to be concrete.

The statement, "Our costs will go up 15 percent this
year if we maintain the present level of overtime," is much
more concrete than, "I want to explore the effect of overtime
on costs." The second statement is appropriate for opening
a conversation whereas the previous statement begins to zero
in on making decisions and evaluating alternatives.

Concreteness is achieved by giving specific examples,
facts, data, and experiences and it is generally reinforced by
being concise and clear. Regarding any given alternative or
course of action, it is possible to stipulate the specific features
or characteristics of that course of action and thereby contribute to concreteness. "Should we buy product X or product
Y?" The answer rests on pinning down the features and bene-

fits of each of these products. As indicated earlier in the decision chart, you cannot make decisions effectively until you begin to specify the characteristics or dimensions of the alternatives under consideration.

Concreteness deals with such things then as "What does it cost?" "What evidence do I have that the alternative is 'doable' or achievable?" "Specifically how does the alternative or course of action under consideration contribute to the achievement of our purposes?" In social situations, if one is trying to decide what to do on a given evening and there are three or four alternatives, clearly those alternatives can be evaluated in a very informal and spontaneous way. However, as one looks back on the evaluation it often involves consideration of cost, satisfaction, and feasibility: "Can we afford to do what we'd like to do?" "Which of the alternatives sounds like it would be most rewarding to us given our present interests and mood? Is the activity (movie, restaurant) available to us?" You contribute to the development of a course of action by being specific about what it is you want to do.

Be Firm and Straightforward Without Being Abrasive or Defensive

Your impact is influenced by the kinds of words you choose. Words like "messy," "careless," "impossible," or "always" create a rigid stance and one which people may feel called upon to resist. For example, an assertive beginning to a problem-solving situation might sound something like, "I am concerned with the quality of work in this area." In contrast, an aggressive or overbearing statement sounds like this: "I am certain that something can be done to improve the quality of work in this department." It is much more appropriate at the outset of a situation to express your confidence in a way which involves other people and does not sound dogmatic or inappropriately unyielding—something like, "I'm confident we can work together to analyze the quality of work in the department and to determine whether or not additional action needs to be taken."

Note that very often when you are "certain" that something can be changed, the other person who is closely involved in the situation may be equally certain that it can't be changed. Therefore, beginning from a position of certainty may block the other person from exploring options and "opening up" to other possibilities. You have lost nothing by being assertive in a developmental and open way even though you may want to become increasingly forceful later on.

Be Convincing/Persuasive

Developing conviction occurs as a result of giving facts which support a given course of action. Once again, describing the features or benefits of a given approach or course of action is a way of building conviction. Closely related to building conviction is the process of persuasion. Persuasiveness and conviction are opposite sides of the same coin. If you want someone to move in a given direction, you achieve this by giving him/her the supporting evidence (conviction) for moving in that direction and by pointing out the benefits (being persuasive) regarding an endeavor. It is not enough simply to describe the features or attributes of the course of action if you want to move toward results; if you want to produce action, then point out benefits.

For example, if you want a raise, it is not sufficient to describe what you have been doing. It is more effective to point out the benefits. Note the contrast. "I've been working hard." "I'm a loyal employee." "I've been working extra hours every night." All of these are descriptions of what you've been doing. They are appropriate in the process of exchanging information. They are not persuasive, however. Persuasive comments communicate benefits to the other person. "By spending a few extra hours each day, I've been able to reorganize the operation to make it more efficient." Or, "I've been spending quite a bit of time with the people who work with me making clear to them some of the advantages of the new program. The result is that they're more cooperative and we're getting better results." These are benefits. they point toward specific outcomes which have value to the other person in the situation and are therefore more likely to persuade that person and produce conviction.

Maintain a "Grounded" Position

Assertiveness calls for a physical stance which is neither rigid and tight nor loose and wishy-washy in order to avoid an inappropriately tentative or inappropriately presumptuous approach to problems. The term "grounded" has been used to describe the physical and emotional sensation and presence which exists within you and is communicated to others when you feel comfortable with yourself. Your sense of confidence or feeling of being grounded is expressed in many ways: by your physical posture, the expression on your face, the look in your eye. Are you standing or sitting rigidly or leaning into the other person in an inappropriately aggressive way? Are you slouched or is your head down indicating to others a lack of inner confidence or discomfort with the situation? Are you looking the other person in the eye without glaring or staring? Are you pointing your finger, clenching your fist, or folding your arms tightly? These and many other indications of your feelings have a profound effect on the degree to which people see you as being ready to problem solve as opposed to taking a win-lose, self-righteous, soft, or compliant position about the issues at hand.

Express Wants and Goals

In the process of making decisions and specifying action it is essential to be sure that your comments and contributions are goal-oriented. It is not enough to say, "I want you to be on time." That statement might be followed with the statement, "It is essential to achieving a smooth running operation and essential to your own contributions to the organization that you be on time. If there are occasions when there is illness or a problem at home, call me as far in advance as possible," or "Our goal is to insure that lateness does not occur and to work out procedures to make sure the job is covered at all times." Indication of the goal places the "want" in the context of the total situation rather than an expression simply of a personal or arbitrary desire.

Set Targets

The expression of wants and goals moves one toward the development of specific targets—measurable, quantitative indications of effectiveness. This is true in relationships between teachers and students, husbands and wives, managers and subordinates. For example, family members may "want" to take a vacation. Their goals may involve relaxation, time away from work. Specific targets must be set if one is to truly engage in assertive-responsive communications.

Statements like "We've agreed that we want to go away next year and we want to be near the ocean. We've examined some alternatives (the lake versus the seashore), we've looked at some of the costs, and we've considered how we feel about each place. Now we can say that we need to set aside $50 a month for the rest of the year in order to go to the Maine seashore next July."

Of course, in day-to-day conversation people do not talk this way. Nevertheless, the process occurs. People sift through what they want. And if they're to achieve results, they set specific targets and mechanisms for achieving them. There-fore, your role as a leader or member of a decision-making group is to contribute and evaluate specific, concrete, convincing and useful information out of which goals and targets can be set. In short, as you move assertively toward specifying what should be done, key behaviors and facilitating techniques include:

1. Support opinions and desires with facts, evidence, and a convincing manner and approach.
2. Be persuasive by going beyond the features of what you want and pointing out the benefits, the advantages, the pay offs, the potential fulfillments of the course of action you recommend.
3. Be sure that before a decision is made your own wants and goals have been made clear and have been built into the process. This does not always mean you get what you want, but it does mean that assertive behavior cannot occur if you are unable or unwilling to express your preferences or to support your views.
4. Strive for clear-cut, measurable, "doable" targets.

Planning Exercise

In order to check out your assertive-responsive skills as they apply to getting what you want, refer back to the means-ends analysis that you completed in Chapter 4 and the alternatives you generated at the bottom of the chart. Alternatively, identify now a specific set of alternatives that you might follow to achieve a purpose of concern to you. Then, in preparation for a future discussion of these alternatives, fill out the planning format that follows.

1. Identify a specific alternative or course of action you want to initiate.

———————————————————————————————

———————————————————————————————

2. Concretely identify relevant facts and features of the course
of action.

_____

_____

3. Prepare to be convincing and persuasive by listing facts which
support the alternative and which indicate the benefits of the
alternative to others.

_____

_____

4. Express your wants and goals regarding the alternative. What
is it that you are really after? What are the conditions you
want to have exist in the future for yourself and for others
involved?

_____

_____

5. Set specific targets. What specific targets do you want to set
in order to move toward the goal or assure implementation
of the alternative you have identified?

_____

_____

Here's an example of a completed planning format. Note
that it is expressed simply as a narrative summary of a person's
thoughts as he/she explores each of the components involved
in specifying actions and making decisions.

Illustrative Example

1. Suppose your chosen alternative is to improve your relationship with another person. First, state your desired course of
action:

   I want to improve my relationship with X.

2. Next, concretely indicate relevant facts and features:

> *I see this person three or four times a day. Operations for which each of us is responsible are related and we have to collaborate quite a bit. We have many mutual working interests: developing our departments, controlling costs, maintaining quality, building our reputations. He/she has a lot of information that's important to me and decisions he/she makes affect the performance of my department. There has been tension between us for some time. Some people see this as a personality conflict. I think it is a product of a competitive situation that has been allowed to build up.*

3. Prepare to be convincing and persuasive by pointing out facts and benefits:

> *Our departments will run more efficiently if we have better information from each other because it will help us in our planning and scheduling of production. This will mean fewer "rush" jobs and down times waiting for products. Smoother production should reduce costs. By exchanging information we should also be able to improve quality and reduce waste. If we can convert the win-lose atmosphere to a win-win, his/her reputation as well as mine has a better chance to benefit.*

4. What are your wants and goals?

> *I want to improve my operation—control or cut costs, improve quality—and build my reputation as a leader and team player. My immediate desire is to establish a better working relationship in order to develop a better source of information for making decisions regarding our two departments.*

5. Set specific targets:

> *My specific targets are (a) to approach the person directly and suggest that we set some goals in this area and (b) to arrange for some informal contacts through attending more meetings together, having lunch together and so on. Specifically, I'm going to suggest that we meet next Tuesday morning to review the relationship between our departments and ways in which it can be improved. I'm going to suggest that we set up a regular series of meetings. However, I'm going to remain open and flexible so that we can develop courses of action which are mutually acceptable and which contribute to our mutual concerns.*

Notice that this same process can be applied im planning a call on a customer if you are a sales representative. You may want to identify your wants and goals, a chosen alternative, the benefits and advantages of that alternative, the specific targets you might set for yourself, etc.—recognizing that this plan may have to be modified after you get together with your sales prospect. This same type of planning can be done in preparation for running a meeting or working more closely with friends or associates on projects of mutual interest

SUMMARY

Assertive-responsive behavior is comprised both of what you do and how you do it. It has been indicated that what you do is enhanced by following specific assertive and responsive patterns while at the same time remaining flexible and engaging others in the problem-solving and decision-making process. The "how to" of assertiveness involves being clear and straightforward and using all of your resources—physical mannerisms, speaking skills, voice, knowledge and experience—to impact on others and to draw them out in ways which contribute to the achievement of specific goals and purposes.

As you pursue these purposes, it is inevitable that in some situations conflict or disagreement will arise. The next chapter deals with the process of defending yourself and achieving goals.

CHAPTER **7**

WE-THEY

DEFENDING YOURSELF

You encounter aggression every day. Although anger is a natural human feeling, many people have trouble directing their anger constructively and affirmatively. The result is that you may find yourself being embarrassed by an unreasonable boss or customer. There may be someone in your work situation who is behaving in ways which are designed to make you look bad or to put you down. On any given day you may encounter aggressive salespeople, managers, taxi drivers, or neighbors. You may find your spouse or friends "blowing their top" at some incident for which you were not to blame. And even in those cases where you have done something to cause another to be hostile, there's always a question as to how much and what kind of aggression you should "sit still for."

For example, if you accidentally step on someone's toe and that person pushes you to the ground and kicks you in the ribs, then it's apparent that you have a right to defend yourself. Similarly, if you unjustly criticize a subordinate's performance in a job situation and that subordinate blows up, calls you names, shouts at you in the presence of others, then you may feel that you have the right to respond even though you were wrong at the outset.

AGGRESSION—EVERY DAY

Whether the incident to which you respond is the result of someone pushing you out of line as you wait for theater tickets, a next-door neighbor violating your property rights, co-workers behaving in an unreasonable or aggressive way, or an argument with your boss, experience has demonstrated to all of us that we must spend considerable time and energy in not only going after what we want but in protecting and defending ourselves from aggression or attacks from others. Competition, win-lose behavior, and a variety of forms of aggression are common in our society. It is not unusual to find teachers who are aggressive toward their students as they rely on hostile criticism, embarrassing comments and often patronizing or contemptuous reactions as a way of dominating the classroom. In business it is common for top managers to "act tough." Doctors, lawyers, cab drivers, and storekeepers often use aggression as a way of "making a point." Here are just a few examples of aggressive statements that you have probably encountered frequently.

> *"I want you to do what you're told and I don't want any arguments." Chances are that you heard this comment as a child and perhaps have heard it, in other forms, much more recently. In some instances the comment may appear to be justified because of your resistance to suggestions or your unwillingness to follow adivce. The fact that it may seem to have been justified does not alter the impact of the statement. It is an aggressive statement. It denies your right to disagree, to "argue," to defend your position. It is dogmatic and fixed. It suggests that the other person knows what is right and you don't. It indicates that in some way or another you don't have the "sense," resources, or experience to deal with the situations you encounter.*
>
> *"Well, you've done it again. You've failed to take responsibility for something I had hoped you were mature enough to handle." You may have heard the statement in a variety of forms. A*

manager may have said to you, "You didn't do what I asked you to. Why can't you follow instructions?" Or a teacher may have said, "You've made the same mistake again. What's the matter with you?" These and dozens of similar statements are aggressive. They suggest you are somehow uncaring or incompetent, that you repeatedly make mistakes.

"Who do you think you are?" "I was here first." "I'm in charge here." "Why should I do it your way?" You may feel in some instances that comments such as these are justified when they are directed at you because you have not been sufficiently understanding, humble, or responsive to the needs and goals of others. Again, this does not change the fact that you have just been dealt with in a hostile and aggressive fashion. Whether you incited this behavior because of your own aggression is an important consideration, but it does not change the fact that you are now called upon to respond to aggression directed at you from someone else.

"Considering the fact that you're inexperienced, you've done a pretty good job." "Considering the fact that you're black, . . ." "Considering the fact that you're a woman, . . ." Although these statements don't appear as obviously aggressive as others, they are examples of condescension or contempt. The implication is that because you're young, or a member of a minority group, or a woman you cannot be expected to perform as intelligently or competently as others. Also, there is an implicit put down in phrases like "You've done pretty well . . ." "considering . . ." and "inexperienced." The second implication is that someone with more competency or from the "right" sex could have done a better job. This denies your resources and discriminates against you.

Regardless of the source of aggression or the causes underlying it, it is essential for every individual to know how to deal with aggression, to be able to defend himself or herself when attacked without escalating the incident. A minor criticism or personal comment may be responded to by a more vigorous or violent attack which in turn results in further recriminations until the individuals involved are engaged in a bitter battle. It is more desirable to behave in ways that reduce the possibility that your behavior will promote further aggression. It is equally desirable to stand up for your beliefs and to avoid being pushed around.

Before pursuing the techniques for defending yourself against overt aggression, it's important to recognize that non-assertive behavior is often equally destructive. There is a close connection between aggressive and nonassertive actions: both are rooted in low self-esteem. Nonassertive behavior is often a manifestation of withheld anger or aggression. By reviewing the nature of nonassertive behavior, you will be in a better position to defend yourself against it.

WATCH OUT FOR THE "NICE GUYS"

Most of us are familiar with the "nice" teacher who is always soft spoken, expresses his/her interest or concern for the children in the classroom, but somehow manages to make them feel inadequate, incompetent and immature. Often the "nice" teacher is unable to express his/her feelings of aggression or frustration and therefore "controls" his/her angry feelings by putting on a false, loving front. Often that front is a cover up for feelings of self-doubt and low self-esteem.

The difficulty is that the underlying feelings of frustration and aggression creep out, often in the form of contemptuous comments and manipulative behavior. For example, picture of soft-spoken, gentle teacher expressing the following feelings in a "loving" or "nice" fashion: "All right boys and girls, I know that it's hard for you to pay attention because your little minds wander and you start thinking about other things. But teacher knows that if you really try, you will be able to understand what I'm going to say." Without extending the example it's clear that the teacher is "putting down" the students. The teacher makes it clear that he/she doesn't have much confidence in their ability to concentrate. The teacher's manner and the content of what is said reinforce the idea that the students are immature, irresponsible, and not very competent. Perhaps without knowing the source of their reactions the students begin to feel they are not capable of making independent decisions or handling complicated ideas. They may become overly dependent on the teacher. In some instances they may find that they feel aggressive and hostile toward the teacher without really knowing why. They begin to feel guilty for their own "unjustified" angry feelings when in reality the teacher's constant condescension justifies that anger.

There are literally dozens of similar examples, ways in which individuals patronize others. For example, very often counselors who are trained to "help" others cover up their own hostility and self-doubt by becoming patronizing. The result is that those being counseled are made to feel less valuable and less competent. Doctors, lawyers and other professionals sometimes use contempt as a weapon for maintaining control in a situation which may frighten them if it escapes their control. Rather than admitting to fear or anger, the doctor may simply show contempt for the patient. This may take the form of expressions of superiority or put downs which demean the knowledge or capacity of the individual patient. Here is a typical incident:

> A patient suffering from coronary disease was consulting a heart surgeon. The patient had read enough to know that there were two basic surgical procedures that might be used in dealing with his particular coronary problem. He asked the surgeon, "Which of the two procedures do you intend to use if you operate on me?" The surgeon responded in a lofty fashion, "Well now, you let me worry about that. You're just a layman

and not in a position to judge technical, surgical procedures. You can be sure that I'll do what's best." These comments were made with a smile and in a somewhat benevolent fashion. The patient felt angry and frustrated. Even though the patient's life was on the line, the "professional" felt that the patient should not question his judgment.

"Nice" behavior, benevolent behavior, paternal behavior is often a way in which another individual can maintain a sense of superiority or maintain control, or in some indirect fashion express his/her hostility or anger toward another without being open about it. The implication is that you have no right to disagree with someone who is speaking in a soft voice or who is expressing affection or concern for your interest. The point is that if that affection or concern is contemptuous and not authentic, if it is a manipulation in order to get you to do something you don't want to, if it is in some form a put down, then clearly you have the right to defend yourself.

STANDING UP FOR YOUR RIGHTS

Assertive and responsive behaviors have been defined as behaviors which are aimed at utilizing your own capacities, defending your own rights, drawing on and engaging the resources of others, and respecting and responding to their rights and capacities. The hard fact is that it is essential for every individual to recognize quickly when his/her rights, resources or individuality are being denied or manipulated. It is essential for every individual to protect his/her own interests without exploiting others and with recognition of the fact that the support, affection and involvement of others are needed.

Expressions such as "defend yourself," "stand up for your

rights," "don't let other people push you around," are some-what misleading in that they suggest a rigid, bristling stance in which the individual is constantly on guard. What is necessary and appropriate is a stance which is resilient and realistic. Taking exception to every comment that seems "slightly off" or constantly looking for aggression or hostility from others is clearly an unhealthy way to relate to the world around you. However, when you are attacked, when you are manipulated, when you are undervalued or patronized, it is necessary and appropriate to respond in affirmative and self-protecting ways. Here are four basic guidelines for dealing both with aggression and nonassertive or guilt-evoking behavior from others:

- ☐ Be straightforward
- ☐ Be responsive
- ☐ Be results-oriented
- ☐ Consider escalation

If someone attacks you, puts you down, or tries to win you over with sympathy or through guilt, these four behaviors will reduce the chance that you will end up feeling uncomfortable about what's going on.

Be Straightforward

There is a strong tendency to "fight fire with fire." The problem with that approach is that often it simply escalates the problem and you find yourself uncomfortable, embarrassed or engaged in a win-lose battle which can do you no good. For example, if someone says to you, "I don't like the way you did this project, you're irresponsible and you don't do anything right," how would you respond? Here are some alternatives. See what you think of them. Place a "+" for statements you feel are OK and a "−" for statements you feel are not OK.

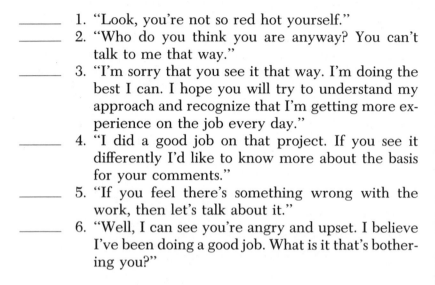

_____ 1. "Look, you're not so red hot yourself."

_____ 2. "Who do you think you are anyway? You can't talk to me that way."

_____ 3. "I'm sorry that you see it that way. I'm doing the best I can. I hope you will try to understand my approach and recognize that I'm getting more experience on the job every day."

_____ 4. "I did a good job on that project. If you see it differently I'd like to know more about the basis for your comments."

_____ 5. "If you feel there's something wrong with the work, then let's talk about it."

_____ 6. "Well, I can see you're angry and upset. I believe I've been doing a good job. What is it that's bothering you?"

You will note that the first two statements are aggressive. They attack the other person, put the person down, challenge the person and, if expressed in a hostile, abrasive tone of voice, they may well incite additional aggression. In some instances an aggressive response may "scare the other person off" and he/she may take a more careful approach in the future. Generally, however, aggressive behavior, particularly if it's directed toward someone who is highly defensive, simply escalates aggression. Note, too, that it is often difficult to act aggressively toward someone who has more power or authority in the system or organization in which you're involved.

The third statement is somewhat apologetic and self-demeaning. It is a nonassertive statement. By behaving in that fashion the individual sets him/herself up for further aggression. So the other individual might go on by saying, "Yeah, well I'm glad you recognize that you're inexperienced and incompetent. I suppose I have to put up with it. Maybe someday you'll be big enough to handle this job." The result is that the individual who is receiving this aggression feels less and less comfortable and in the long run may explode with anger or simply leave the situation. In a work situation this kind of behavior might encourage employees to quit or file a grievance with a union, or to join a union if there is one.

The next two statements (4 and 5) are straightforward and assertive. They also show a willingness to interact. The individual states his/her point of view rather than "knuckling under," apologizing or attacking. At the same time, however, there is nothing in the statements which is self-demeaning or which in any way reduces the rights or resources of the individual taking such a stance. The last statement (6) begins with an empathetic assertion; that is, it demonstrates awareness of "where the other person is coming from." The statement also includes an assertive component and a question. It is neither evaluative nor apologetic. It is both assertive and responsive. This leads to the second reaction which is effective in defending yourself against aggressive actions and attitudes or nonassertive manipulations.

Be Responsive

When someone is arguing with you, your chances of clarifying the argument or resolving it are greatly enhanced if you find out more about the nature of the argument. What is the person saying or feeling? Why does the person believe and feel that way? What basis does the individual have for the statement being made? What are his/her perceptions and assumptions about the situation? In addition, when confronted with aggression, responsiveness diffuses or reduces that aggression and the aggressor sees it is not necessary to be hostile, vindictive or defensive. Similarly, when someone is behaving nonasser-

tively, a responsive comment draws the person out. By showing some awareness of the other person's feelings without
demeaning your own position, you open up the potential for
problem solving. Note statement 6 includes an assertive or
straightforward comment and a responsive reaction which
may elicit clarification and enhance the chances of solving
the problem.

It's important to recognize, too, that very often you are
dealing with individuals who have more power or authority
than you do. It may be very difficult to obtain results or to
defend yourself effectively if you rely only on aggression or
assertiveness as your major weapon or tool for dealing with
powerful opponents. For example, if your boss says, "I think
you're careless and sloppy," it's doubtful whether you feel
free to go back and say, "Well, you're pretty careless and
sloppy yourself so why don't you shut up." It is more likely
that you might take a firm stand by saying, "I think I'm doing
a good job." (assertive) "What's wrong?" (responsive)

When faced with superior power and aggression it may
be appropriate to make a straightforward, assertive statement
or to combine assertiveness with responsiveness so as to provide some opportunity to resolve the situation without demeaning or embarrassing yourself and without getting physically or psychologically damaged. Often the best reaction is
a purely responsive comment such as, "Tell me more about
what's bothering you" or "What happened that made you
angry?"

In dealing with persons who have less power than you
do, or who are peers (physically, psychologically or organiza-
tionally) it is still appropriate to behave responsively. For example, suppose you are an experienced manager in a large
office and a new, young clerk was embarrassed or upset by
something you said and responded by saying, "Just because
you're the boss doesn't mean you can push me around. As
far as I'm concerned you're just a snob and a management
fink and I don't care what you say." Responding with aggres-

sion not only would have little effect in solving this problem, it might also distract from your own sense of well-being and confidence and from the respect which you wish to maintain in dealing with other people. Clearly you could take a hard but straightforward assertive stance, possibly calling the person aside to say, "Your inability to deal with this problem in a straightforward way, the fact that you shouted out personal insults in public, is a serious problem. I can understand that you were upset; however, if this happens again, you'll be terminated." Alternatively you might be responsive, "I want to understand the basis for your reaction today." Compare these approaches with shouting back to the individual on the office floor, "I don't know who you think you are. You're just a loud mouth. If you ever say anything like that again, I'll personally throw you out."

Which of these comments would leave the manager with self-respect, a good feeling about handling the problem, and with the respect of those in the office? The aggressive approach would create a lot of attention but the chances are it would not increase the maturity, openness and respect of the work group.

In this connection it's important to recognize that in many instances when you are in a position of authority or power, your behavior becomes a model for others. For example, parents, teachers, and managers who engage in abusive and aggressive behavior simply set up a model or standard for others whom they guide to do likewise. Gradually, the individuals learn that the "style" of the family, group, or organization is to "scream" or to become abusive with each other. That style begins to dominate the family unit or organization. This is not to suggest that you should never lose your temper or express your feelings. If someone insults you, it may be appropriate to raise your voice or to be very strong and forthright in expressing your feelings, but this response need not be aggressive.

Consider, again, the example of the office manager who

was abused by the clerk. The manager might respond to the clerk, "You said some personal things that make me angry. I don't like what you said and I don't feel it should have been said here." A responsive comment frequently makes it possible to resolve the problem without taking final or destructive action. So the same statement might be more acceptable if the manager said, "What you've said makes me very angry. I don't understand 'where you're coming from.' I want you to come to my office and I want to hear what this is about." Suggesting that you want to "hear what this is about" is a responsive comment indicating that you are available to listen even though you are angry.

Be Results-Oriented

In many instances the solution of interpersonal problems is enhanced if the parties involved are clear about their objective. An objective is "a condition that you wish to have exist in the future." If someone gets angry with you and you are able to think through your response, you may wish to ask yourself:

> *"How do I want this to end? Do I want it to end by the person being increasingly angry with me or by my becoming abusive with him/her? Do I want it to end by my feeling that I've been outgunned or out-manipulated? Do I want to punish the person? Or, do I want it to end by solving a problem and/or improving a relationship?"*

In most cases the last response is the most desirable alternative. Generally, individuals become aggressive out of their own fear, anger or confusion. Your goal as a co-worker, manager, friend or subordinate is not to fight a battle with the other person. Rather, you want to resolve the problem without demeaning yourself or reducing your own sense of worth and effectiveness. A great many interpersonal squabbles can be handled more quickly and successfully if one or both of the parties address themselves to the problem, to the results rather than to personal invective.

For example, assume that someone who works directly for you comes to you and says, "I think I'm being treated unfairly. You're unreasonable and you're never willing to listen to anybody." Obviously, the individual is angry. If you are in a position of authority, it may be tempting simply to "straighten the person out." However, if your goal is to solve the problem, you may want to stress results rather than personal reactions. Accordingly, you might say, "I can see that you're angry and frankly I don't really know what it is that has caused you to feel this way. What's this about?" This response does not demean either yourself or the other person. You've indicated a willingness to explore what has happened and how the other person feels. There is a likelihood that the other individual will respond by reducing his/her hostility and begin to address the issue. The real problem may be that the person wants more freedom, more authority, more money, more opportunity to contribute, better assignments, and so on. You have a better chance of achieving something useful by shifting the focus to a results-orientation rather than simply wasting time and energy in a personal battle.

Note that assertive-responsive modes of action never suggest that you should demean yourself, ignore your own feelings or withhold or repress those feelings simply to make someone else more comfortable or more happy. The goal is to be straightforward, responsive and to move toward results rather than into a battle.

Consider Escalation

There are times when it is appropriate to escalate; that is, to move up the scale of reaction, to be more assertive, to use whatever power you have available to solve the problem.

Escalation may occur simply by attacking the other person before he/she attacks you.

Suppose a student says to a teacher, "Listen, I'm sick of your lectures. As far as I'm concerned you don't know what's going on and you're . . ." The teacher may escalate by pointing out negative consequences or by using punishment or sanctions as a way of resolving the issue: "You've said some things which are not only wrong but I find personally objectionable. If you make one more comment you'll be suspended." Notice, however, that when you escalate into stronger actions or even into aggression, you reduce the chance of an amicable or useful resolution of the problem. Generally you simply "put out the fire."

However, if the straightforward and responsive approaches don't work, if you're unable to solve the problem by working in a results-oriented way, you may want to escalate into negative consequences or even into aggression.

JUSTIFIED AGGRESSION

There is a genuine question as to whether aggression is ever justified. For example, if someone insults you, is it justified to insult that person back? If someone demeans your capacity, should you demean theirs? Most of the suggestions and examples presented earlier emphasize that you will generally make more progress by being straightforward rather than aggressive. You can express your feelings, you can be clear about your anger or dissatisfaction without attacking the other person's background, calling names, or reducing the battle to a verbal contest. You can be responsive and indicate a concern for the other person's point of view even as you make it clear that you don't intend to accept or knuckle under to aggressive behavior.

You can use power or energy when it's available and

escalate beyond simply stating your point of view and feelings. You may, for example, threaten someone. Suppose you're returning damaged merchandise to a store and a clerk or supervisor becomes aggressive. You then indicate your dissatisfaction because of that aggression. If you still are unable to resolve the problem, you may choose to escalate by saying, "If this isn't settled to my satisfaction I intend to retain a lawyer" or "to report this to the Better Business Bureau." Notice that these escalations, by definition, occur after a genuine endeavor has been made to solve the problem and to express your own views without hostility.

You can accomplish almost everything you want to accomplish by using assertive and responsive statements and, if necessary, by escalating through reference to negative consequences. Suggesting possible negative consequences—that someone may be suspended or terminated, that you plan to report a given occurrence to a professional society or Better Business Bureau, that a person in authority (the boss, mother, father) will object to the individual's behavior—is not aggressive behavior. Many discussions of when one should be aggressive become confusing because individuals mistake strong affirmative action for aggression. Throughout this book a distinction has been drawn between assertive and aggressive behavior. Being firm and strong, using information—including information which points out negative consequences—to solve problems, is not aggressive. Letting people know what you feel and believe, even with a strong expression of negative feeling, is not aggressive. Putting others down is.

The only justification for aggression is: for survival or for "shock value." Perhaps one of the clearest examples of appropriate aggressive behavior has been dramatized in plays and movies over and over again. Someone in a crisis situation suddenly begins behaving hysterically. Some other character in the play, usually the hero, slaps the person across the face. The person in hysterics is jarred from the hysterical and unproductive behavior and shocked into more useful or appropriate action. Slapping someone across the face is certainly an aggressive act, yet it may be—even in real life as well as in drama— an appropriate way of shocking the other person into a more realistic orientation to the problem at hand. It may be a necessary step for survival.

Verbal aggression may play a similar role. Often in "street situations" a strong, aggressive statement may be necessary to make it clear that you plan to defend yourself. It may be necessary as a way of surviving in the street. It may also be a way of shocking people into positive action. Teachers, counselors, therapists, doctors, and managers are at times able to use aggression skillfully and knowledgeably as a way of shaking people into a new awareness regarding a specific problem or situation.

This was reflected very clearly in a labor-management negotiation over a new contract between a company and a union. In the eyes of the union, management had taken a very hard position and very little progress was being made. People seemed to be dodging issues and unwilling to confront the real problems. Finally, at one point, one of the negotiators for the union side spoke up and said, "I've been sitting here listening for the last two hours and as far as I'm concerned the management negotiating team is behaving as though they don't give a damn about anybody. There are people out there who aren't getting paychecks, who aren't getting enough to eat. I think you guys are simply exploiting this situation without concern for anybody but yourselves." The negotiator was aggressive, hostile, abusive in his manner and in what he said. The immediate management reaction was aggressive. However, the exchange broke through the political double talk that had been going on and after some heat the individuals were able to get to work and reach a settlement. In short, there are times when aggression is appropriate as a last defense or as a way of shaking people into action.

CONCLUSIONS

In day-to-day interactions with people it is essential to deal with aggressiveness and nonassertiveness effectively. Individuals must know how to defend their rights and how to utilize their resources in pursuing goals and career objectives. The key requirements for effectiveness are to be straightforward, results-oriented, and responsive and to have the knowledge and skills to escalate your reactions appropriately. Aggressive or nonassertive behavior are rarely useful in dealing with people.

In the final chapter you will find a summary of key skills and a guide for planning for self-improvement.

CHAPTER **8**

PLANNING FOR
SELF-IMPROVEMENT

In every area of activity successful people strive to improve themselves. Professional athletes continuously try to obtain feedback and strive to improve their performance. Surgeons and effective managers keep up-to-date on new practices and techniques by reading and attending seminars. They, too, obtain feedback and analysis from others. Recent United States presidents have utilized teachers, consultants and experts in various fields to provide them with feedback and training to strengthen their public speaking skills, their capacity to handle press conferences, their capacity to cope with complex economic and international issues. It is desirable and usually possible for most of us to obtain instruction from books and courses and guidance and feedback from friends, associates, and others experienced in our fields of interest. In planning your own self-development, these resources should be tapped as a major aid to self-analysis and improvement.

ONLY YOU CAN CHANGE

It is, however, a serious mistake to assume that others can change you. People change and improve if and when *they choose* to change and improve. Although you can obtain guidance, counseling and instruction, only you can take the specific actions necessary to improve your own effectiveness and performance. There are three steps in the self-improvement process:

1. Become aware of your current level of effectiveness.
2. Establish goals and expectations for improvement.
3. Develop and practice the skills required to reach your goals.

In earlier chapters, checklists have been used to aid you in identifying areas where improvement is desired. In the Self-Improvement Planning Guide which follows you will find a more thorough set of self-assessment devices and a format for setting goals and expectations. The key skills for achieving results in each of these areas are also identified.

SELF-IMPROVEMENT
PLANNING GUIDE

In Section I of this guide you will find a list of key behaviors which can be used to aid you in moving toward your specific goals. For example, if you want to sell your ideas more effectively to associates or managers, you may need to learn how to be more enthusiastic and more persuasive. If you want to improve your ability to handle conflict, you may have to increase your capacity to be resilient and at the same time to be a good listener and respond to other people. These and similar patterns of behavior are identified in the paragraphs which follow under Section I. In Section II you are asked to rate yourself in each of these areas, thus identifying improvement goals. In Section III you will summarize your ratings in each area, pin down your improvement goals, and review the "how to's" to form a basis for specific action.

SECTION I—ASSERTIVE AND RESPONSIVE BEHAVIOR

Here are specific modes of behavior associated with assertiveness. These will be followed by the modes associated with responsiveness. First, become familiar with each of these modes. Then you will be able to assess how assertive and responsive you are and the areas which might be strengthened.

Assertive Modes

Informative-Straightforward

Informative communication occurs when the communicator's behavior is:

☐ Firm and clear (not highly tentative or equivocal).

☐ Based on facts; opinions are expressed briefly and without prejudice.

☐ Usually succinct; short, clear sentences—well-defined ideas.

Enthusiastic

Enthusiasm is basically an outward expression of excitement and concern. Enthusiasm is communicated when the communicator's behavior is:

☐ Animated through physical movement, a "grounded" body posture with head up, without high tension, nervousness or inappropriately relaxed behavior; gestures are natural and related to the ideas being expressed.

☐ Varied through voice dynamics. Often enthusiasm is coupled with somewhat louder than usual conversation and changes in volume and pitch. Delivery is sometimes rapid but not frenzied.

Forceful

Forcefulness and impact are achieved through:

- ☐ Strong eye contact—direct, not glaring, staring, darting, avoiding.
- ☐ Ideas supported by facts—often deliberate with heavy emphasis on key ideas.
- ☐ "Grounded" body posture—straightforward gestures, no slouching, direct face-to-face stance.
- ☐ Voice and expression are firm and positive—at times voice level may be low but firm and distinct, affirmative, unequivocal expressions are used—no apologies.

Persuasive

Persuasive behavior is behavior which moves other people toward a goal or interest that the speaker wishes to achieve. Thus, the speaker sells ideas, points of view, etc. Key ingredients are:

- ☐ Talks benefits; that is, expresses clearly advantages and payouts to the other person.
- ☐ Uses positive, affirmative words and phrases.
- ☐ Usually includes elements considered under enthusiasm (animation, voice dynamics, etc.).

Controlling

At times a forceful, firm position needs to be coupled with clear indications that the individual will not "permit" deviations from a prescribed course of action. This involves more than selling ideas. In many instances it includes an attempt to impose a given course of action on another individual, often in that person's best interest (for example, warning a child that he/she may be burned by a hot stove). Control is communicated by:

□ Pointing out negative sanctions or negative consequences.
□ Using the behaviors associated with forcefulness—particularly strong body posture and eye contact. Using authority or power as available.

Responsive Modes

Empathetic

Empathy requires the capacity to tune into the feelings and concerns of other people. Manifestations of empathy include:

□ Picking up and expressing feelings present in others (for example, I can see you feel upset).
□ Adapting or adjusting manner, stance and voice to the feelings of the other.
□ Setting aside (temporarily) own immediate goals in order to be responsive to the other.

Active Listener

Listening is more than simply remaining silent. It involves demonstrating to the other person that you've heard what he/she says. Using empathy and appropriate questions or summaries to stay tuned in and understand the views of the other is desirable. Behaviors include:

☐ Using open questions (avoid district attorney-like attacks or probes).

☐ Using reflective responses or feeding back to the other person his/her understanding of the other's view.

☐ Using summary statements.

☐ Maintaining good eye contact.

☐ Showing patience and openness to other's viewpoints.

☐ Remaining silent or encouraging the other person to talk.

Catalytic

One of the skills in engaging other individuals involves the capacity to facilitate their involvement. In group and social situations a catalyst is someone who makes it possible for other people to act or interact. Behaviors include:

☐ Using listening skills.

☐ Identifying goals expressed by others and getting the views of others "on the table."

☐ Encouraging the exploration of alternatives.

☐ Acting as a gatekeeper; that is, getting other people in and out of the conversation by asking questions, repeating their ideas, putting things on a blackboard.

☐ Picking up or expressing thoughts and ideas that have not yet been clarified but are present in the minds of others.

Warmth

People who are able to create a warm or friendly feeling often get better information, more support, more involvement from other people. Warmth is expressed by:

☐ Applying and demonstrating empathy.

☐ Applying and demonstrating listening skills.

☐ Showing a willingness to express positive, warm feelings.

☐ Being receptive and comfortable with the warm feelings and concerns of others.

Sincere

Responsiveness is enhanced when one is believed; when one has credibility. Sincerity reflects your genuine concern, interests and availability to others. Key behaviors are:

☐ Genuinely listening and expressing warmth.

☐ Showing feelings straightforwardly without putting people down or evoking guilt.

☐ Using information straightforwardly without distortion or prejudice.

SECTION II—SELF-RATING

Given these brief descriptions and key elements of assertive and responsive behavior, you are now asked to "rate yourself." Each of the major modes of assertive and responsive activity will be identified along with a brief summary statement. You may want to refer back to the Section I descriptions to clarify further each component. Use a scale of 1 through 5 to rate yourself. The scale is described briefly below:

1. Needs immediate and significant improvement.
2. Improvement definitely needed.
3. Doing pretty well in this area. Some improvement desirable.
4. This is not a major area of concern. I'm doing well. I could and should improve a bit in this area.
5. I'm doing great in this area. No significant improvement required.

After each of the assertive and responsive modes expressed below, rate yourself 1 through 5.

Assertive Modes

_____ Informative—straightforward
I express myself clearly and straightforwardly. People have told me that I'm easy to understand. I am rarely accused of talking too much or holding information back. I don't exaggerate, apologize or distort information very often.

_____ Enthusiastic
I express myself openly and expansively. I show excitement and interest. People have told me that I do create excitement and stimulate their involvement. I'm known as a person who gets "charged up" about things.

_____ Forceful
When I want something I make it very clear to others and they know exactly what I have in mind. I'm seen as someone who has strength, who is able and willing to express his/her viewpoints with emphasis and clarity. I'm not overbearing or unreasonable in pushing for what I want.

_____ Persuasive
I use my enthusiasm and sometimes my forcefulness to sell ideas to other people to get them to move in a direction which I think is desirable. I create interest in others by successfully pointing out the benefits of a course of action, by selling my position without becoming overbearing. People tell me that I have a way of getting things done with others, stimulating their interest and getting their support.

_____ Controlling

When I need to I can really put on the pressure without putting people down or becoming nasty. I'm willing to confront negative possibilities. For example, if someone working for me isn't performing well, I tell them they may not get promoted or they may not get an expected raise in pay if they don't improve their performance. If one of my children or associates is destructive or hostile, I make it clear that that behavior is not acceptable and there will be negative consequences if it continues. People see me as strong and resilient under pressure rather than brittle or "hard-nosed."

Responsive Modes

_____ Empathetic

I find it quite easy to understand the feelings of other people. I know when they're upset, angry, "down," or "up." People tell me that I seem to have unusual insight and sensitivity to the needs and concerns of others. I am able to tune in.

_____ Active Listener

I actively strive to understand other people's points of view. I ask questions. When appropriate I remain silent or feed back what I have heard to try to clarify and show understanding. People have told me that I'm a good listener.

_____ Catalytic

I am able in many sitautions to put aside my own immediate self-interests and to make it possible for other people to get involved or engaged in what's going on. I do this sometimes by asking questions or by supporting the views of others to be sure they get listened to. People tell me that when I'm involved in a problem-solving situation or relating to another person things happen. People don't stay passive or uninterested.

_____ Warm
I am frequently able to feel and express positive and affectionate feelings to people around me. I am interested in people and concerned with what's happening. People tell me that I'm warm, humanistic, "nice to be around."

_____ Sincere
I express my views straightforwardly without apologies and without exaggeration. I want people to know what I truly think and feel and where I stand. I have a natural, straightforward manner in dealing with people. They don't feel I'm "putting them on" or trying to impress them or control the situation. People tell me that I'm credible, reliable, someone they feel they can trust.

SECTION III—PLANNING FOR IMPROVEMENT

Analysis of Improvement Areas

In the following Self-Improvement Analysis you will find three columns. The first column is utilized to record your "score;" that is, your current level of performance. The next column should be used to state briefly "where you want to be"—statements such as, "I want to be more straightforward, more dynamic, more open to the ideas of others, etc." are appropriate to aid you in thinking through your own improvement plans. In the third column, utilize information provided in Sections

SELF-IMPROVEMENT ANALYSIS

	Where You Are	Where You Want to Be	How to Get There
ASSERTIVE			
Informative	_____	_____	_____
		_____	_____
Enthusiastic	_____	_____	_____
		_____	_____
Forceful	_____	_____	_____
		_____	_____
Persuasive	_____	_____	_____
		_____	_____
Controlling	_____	_____	_____
		_____	_____
RESPONSIVE			
Empathetic	_____	_____	_____
		_____	_____
Listener	_____	_____	_____
		_____	_____
Catalytic	_____	_____	_____
		_____	_____
Warm	_____	_____	_____
		_____	_____
Sincere	_____	_____	_____
		_____	_____

I and II to *specify the actions you intend to take to get where you want to go.*

For example, if you gave yourself a score of "2" on forcefulness, and then indicated that you have a desire to be more forceful in dealing with family members or associates, you should then indicate specific actions—drawing particularly on the checklist in Section I. Perhaps to be more forceful you want to try to be more concise, more deliberate, more willing to express your viewpoints clearly and straightforwardly.

Using the format that follows, identify "where you stand" using the scores in Section II. In your own interests and based on your own beliefs, indicate where you want to be. Finally, identify specific action steps—the specific behaviors—that you can begin employing. Later on in this chapter there will be opportunities to develop more specific action plans. Right now the goal is to identify the behaviors that you wish to strengthen.

Making Plans

Based on the preceding Self-Improvement Analysis, you have indicated areas in which you feel you can be more effective. Some of the specific actions or behaviors associated with these changes have also been identified.

Thus, you may have found from experience and through completion of the checklist that you are not coming across as sincere or straightforward. You may have known earlier that you are not as forceful or enthusiastic as you would like. But now you may have identified some of those things that have to happen in order for you to be more of whatever it is you wish to be.

The key question now is how to begin improving or changing in these areas. As indicated earlier, it is desirable to get feedback, suggestions and counseling from others as appropriate. Your friends, associates and other experienced and professional individuals with whom you deal may be able to give you some suggestions and ideas as well as feedback as to how you're coming across. Ultimately, however, you must take action on your own. Here are some specific action plans that you might consider.

Self-improvement through audiotape or videotape practice.
One way of improving your voice dynamics, sharpening up
the directness or succinctness of your comments or ideas is
to record your own voice and listen back. After listening and
reviewing the checklist provided earlier, as well as your own
experience, record yourself again, this second time trying to
be more succinct, more straightforward, more forceful using
shorter phrases if that's appropriate or expanding the dynamics of your voice.

If you or a friend have a videotape recorder or camera
available, this is an even better way of seeing yourself in action.
Although these items are expensive, many companies have
them available so that your employer may permit you to tape
yourself. Audio and videotape recorders are sometimes available at public schools or at an adult education course. There
are many opportunities to hear and see yourself in action
through the use of tape. Use the tape not only to feed back
and criticize but also to practice and revise your behavior
in line with your goals.

Use of planning techniques. As indicated in earlier chapters,
the best way to get somewhere is to be clear about where
you want to go. If you want to improve or change your behavior, it is useful to *write down* some of your behavioral goals.
For example, if you want to be more forceful, think of a situation that you are about to face and plan out that situation.
Identify specific goals, use the formats from earlier chapters
and be clear about where you're going and how you plan to
get there.

You can begin practicing assertive-responsiveness skills
in "low risk" situations. Thus, if you want to be more forceful
and demanding, it is probably not a wise idea to make your
first effort in this area in dealing with a top executive in the
company where you work or with a policeman who pulls you
over for speeding. However, it is certainly useful and practical
to practice your forcefulness in returning merchandise to a

store or arguing with friends or relatives about issues that are of concern to you.

Recognize that there is a clear-cut distinction between being forceful and being abrasive or aggressive. If in trying out new and more forceful behavior with friends or associates you get "negative feedback" or if people become highly argumentative and angry, then you know that you need to continue practicing and to "lighten up" and use your responsive skills more carefully.

In any case, your chances of improving are much better if you determine specifically what it is you want to accomplish and plan some of your comments to see how they work. Perhaps you have a friend with whom you may argue about a given sports team or a political issue or a social issue. Assume you know that some time in your next conversation you will probably discuss the performance of a given football team or the use of nuclear power or some other issue of concern to both of you. *Plan key points that you wish to make.* Think of ways you can make them more pointedly, more forcefully.

The same kind of practice can occur—as you feel more comfortable with the process—in dealing with people on the job, with managers, subordinates, union members and officials. It is important to recognize that practice is not play acting. It is deciding what you want to do and doing it.

Put yourself in a new situation. One of the problems that many people encounter is that they never have a chance to try out more persuasive communication or to improve their listening skills. Depending on your interests, there is a wide range of possibilities for improving your assertive-responsive behavior. It might be useful to take on a part-time job as a sales representative in order to practice more persuasive communications. There are many part-time positions in retail stores or in house-to-house canvassing which offer opportunities to "reach out" and practice more assertive behavior. You might want to join a discussion group or a public speaking group. Those who work might request some kind of a small-group activity, joining a committee or serving on some discussion group. Certainly there are innumerable opportunities to practice responsive skills in dealing with spouses, with children, with teachers and business people.

You can practice assertive and responsive approaches in many social situations. Try mirroring back your understanding of the points of view of others. Active listening methods are often extremely useful in getting to know people. Assume you have just met someone new and are seated with that person at a restaurant. There is time to fill and a need to talk. After some initial conversation the individual brings up something of interest. Rather than immediately responding with your own viewpoint, try finding out more about the other's viewpoint. Do this consciously and specifically by rephrasing what the other person has said or by asking a direct question. For example, if the other person says, "I'm convinced that Mr. X would make a good representative on the school board," you might say (rather than expressing your own view about Mr. X), "I'd like to hear more about your feelings about Mr. X."

Here is a list of "new situations" that you might consider entering into in order to put yourself in a position to practice assertive-responsive skills and to become more effective in dealing with people and with a larger range of experiences and opportunities.

☐ Education courses—adult education, high school equivalency, college courses.

☐ Community endeavors—attending school board meetings, planning or zoning meetings, participating in fund-raising drives, Red Cross, etc.

☐ Taking on a leadership role—offering to be a chairperson at an important meeting or take over a district in getting voters out or heading up a committee.

☐ Service organizations—any number of institutions, clubs, lodges, chambers of commerce, trade associations, unions which you can join or in which you can become more actively involved.

☐ New work assignments—request new or varied assignments, join committees, attend after hours training sessions.

This is, of course, only a partial list of the kinds of activities which give you an opportunity to improve your communication skills. One of the ways of becoming more assertive is to "get into things." Speak out at management meetings, union meetings, town meetings. Stand up and clearly express your views in social and business situations. Clearly, when actions of this type are done in a pompous, belligerent or prideful manner they distract from your effectiveness. Assertiveness is more than simply acting. It is acting in response to the concerns and feelings of others. Responsiveness is sensitivity for the situation in which you are involved. This means, then, that you need to practice simultaneously both assertiveness and responsiveness.

CONCLUSION

In order to get better at anything you have to act. In order to make your actions meaningful and constructive you need to get feedback, to assess how things are going, and to experiment with new modes of behavior. No one can change you, improve you, train you or modify your behavior. Others can give you information, feedback, make suggestions, set up exercises, formulate plans or evaluate your performance. *However, only you can act on what you learn from the people and situations you encounter.*

In order to expand in directions which are important to you, you also need to expand the opportunities to try out new behavior, to learn more about yourself, to get more feedback and to get more practice. This book has been aimed at suggesting ways in which you can clarify your goals and plan for improvement. It has suggested specific action steps you can take to build upon your resources and move toward your goals. It has suggested that only you can decide what to do and when to do it.

You have the capacity to make things happen. Although thinking, planning, discussing, reading and wondering are all useful elements in the process of self-improvement, nothing happens until you act.

SUGGESTED READINGS

Alberti, Robert E. *Assertiveness: Innovations, Applications, Issues.* San Luis Obispo, Calif.: Impact, 1977.

Alberti, R. E., & Emmons, M. L. *Stand Up, Speak Out, Talk Back.* New York: Simon and Schuster, Inc., August, 1975.

Alberti, R. E., & Emmons, M. L. *Your Perfect Right: A Guide to Assertive Behavior.* San Luis Obispo, Calif.: Impact, 1974.

Bach, George R., & Goldberg, Herb. *Creative Aggression: A Guide to Assertive Living.* New York: Avon, 1974.

Calvert, C. How to get what you want and keep it. *Mademoiselle.* March, 1975.

Dyer, Wayne. *Your Erroneous Zones.* New York: Funk & Wagnalls, 1976.

Eisler, R. M., et al. Components of assertive behavior. *Journal of Clinical Psychology,* 1973.

Fensterheim, H. Behavior Therapy: Assertive Training in Groups. In C. Sager & H. Kaplan (Eds.). *Progress in Group and Family Therapy.* New York: Brunner/Mazel, 1972.

Fensterheim, H., & Baer, Jean. *Don't Say Yes When You Want to Say No.* New York: Dell, 1975.

Friedman, P. H. The effects of modeling and role-playing on assertive behavior. In R. D. Rubin, H. Fensterheim, A. A. Lazarus & C. M. Franks (Eds.). *Advances in Behavior Therapy.* New York: Academic Press, 1971.

Harris, Thomas A., M.D. *I'm OK—You're OK: A Practical Guide to Transactional Analysis.* New York: Harper & Row, 1969.

Jakubowski-Spector, P. Self-assertion training procedures for women. In D. Carter & E. Rawlings (Eds.), *Psychotherapy for Women: Treatment Towards Equality.* Springfield, Illinois: Charles C Thomas, 1975.

James, M., & Jongeward, D. *Born to Win: Transactional Analysis with Gestalt Experiments.* Reading, Mass.: Addison-Wesley, 1971.

Newman, Mildred, & erkowitz, Bernard. *How to Be Your Own Best Friend.* New York: Ballantine, 1974.

Serber, M. Teaching the nonverbal components of assertive training. *Journal of Behavior Therapy and Experimental Psychiatry,* 1972.

Shaw, Malcolm E. *Assertive-Responsive Management: A Personal Handbook.* Reading, Mass.: Addison-Wesley, 1979.

Smith, Manuel J., Ph.D. *When I Say No, I Feel Guilty.* Bantam Books, 1975.

Wolpe-Lazarus Assertiveness Questionnaire: Wolpe, J., & Lazarus A. A. *Behavior Therapy Techniques.* New York: Pergamon Press, 1966.